T0358537

ROUTLEDGE LIBRARY EDITIONS: EMPLOYMENT AND UNEMPLOYMENT

Volume 7

UNEMPLOYMENT

UNEMPLOYMENT

The European Perspective

Edited by
ANGUS MADDISON AND BOTE S. WILPSTRA

Routledge
Taylor & Francis Group

LONDON AND NEW YORK

First published in 1982 by Croom Helm Ltd

This edition first published in 2019
by Routledge
2 Park Square, Milton Park, Abingdon, Oxon OX14 4RN

and by Routledge
52 Vanderbilt Avenue, New York, NY 10017

Routledge is an imprint of the Taylor & Francis Group, an informa business

British Library Cataloguing in Publication Data
A catalogue record for this book is available from the British Library

ISBN: 978-1-138-38855-0 (Set)
ISBN: 978-0-429-02498-6 (Set) (ebk)
ISBN: 978-0-367-02733-9 (Volume 7) (hbk)
ISBN: 978-0-429-39812-4 (Volume 7) (ebk)

Publisher's Note
The publisher has gone to great lengths to ensure the quality of this reprint but
points out that some imperfections in the original copies may be apparent.

Disclaimer
The publisher has made every effort to trace copyright holders and would welcome
correspondence from those they have been unable to trace.

UNEMPLOYMENT
THE EUROPEAN PERSPECTIVE

EDITED BY ANGUS MADDISON AND BOTE S. WILPSTRA

CROOM HELM
London & Canberra

British Library Cataloguing in Publication Data

Unemployment.
   1. Unemployment—European Economic Community
countries—Congresses
   I. Maddison, Angus   2. Wilpstra, Bote
   331.13'794   HD5715.5.E/

   ISBN 0-7099-1739-2

Printed and bound in Great Britain by
Biddles Ltd, Guildford and King's Lynn

CONTENTS

FOREWORD

Unemployment was a major scourge of the advanced capitalist countries in the 1930s, but in the golden age of postwar expansion which lasted for a quarter century until 1973, it had seemingly been vanquished by enlightened economic policy. Since 1973, unemployment has reemerged as a major problem, along with accelerated inflation, and problems of structural adjustment imposed by soaring energy prices.

The rise in European unemployment came in two surges as a result of the generalised recessions in 1974-5 and 1980-81. At end 1981, unemployment in the European Community is running close to 9 per cent of the labour force compared with a "norm" of under 2 per cent in the 1960s.

These rather abrupt and serious changes in the labour market situation have created major new dilemmas for economic policy and have stirred significant and acrimonious theoretical controversy.

For this reason, the University of Groningen felt it would be useful to hold an international symposium to analyse both the policy issues and the academic debate in a comparative perspective. In the Netherlands, academic and official discussion has had a rather special flavour with heavier emphasis on structural problems than elsewhere. Because of this, it was felt that a confrontation between Dutch economists and those from other countries could perhaps throw a new light on some of the issues.

The present volume contains some of the papers from our September 1980 conference. There are three comparative papers on the employment policy discussion in Germany, the Netherlands and the U.K. as well as papers examining the theoretical adequacy of Keynesian, monetarist, structuralist and Marxist reactions to the new issues. The papers are all accompanied by a critique from the discussants. A companion volume Unemployment: A Dutch Perspective, Ministry of Social Affairs, the Hague, 1982 includes five papers illustrating the full range of contemporary policy approaches and theoretical controversies in the Netherlands, as well as a paper on the prewar unemployment problem and policy debate.

We wish to express our gratitude for financial support from the Groningen Economics Faculty, The Netherlands Bank, and the Ministry of Social Affairs. We are grateful to the World Bank for facilitating the participation of Deepak Lal, and would like to express our appreciation to our colleagues Simon Kuipers and Joan Muysken in the organisation of the meeting.

Angus Maddison
Bote Wilpstra

THE UNEMPLOYMENT POLICY DISCUSSION IN THE U.K. IN THE 1970s

M.FG. Scott, Nuffield College, Oxford.

What Has Happened

The full employment era in the U.K. lasted from the Second World War until 1966. As can be seen from Table 1, it was characterised by a low unemployment rate, moderate inflation, and a rate of growth of the gross domestic product which, while low by the international standards of the time, was high by the U.K.'s own historical standards.

After 1966 the situation deteriorated, with unemployment rising and inflation accelerating. After 1973, it became even worse, and now the rate of growth also slowed down. Since 1976 the unemployment percentage has remained above 5 and, by mid-1981, had climbed to above 10, the highest since the 1930's. The rate of growth of retail prices reached nearly 25 per cent per annum in 1975, was brought down to about 8 per cent per annum in 1978 by a temporarily successful incomes policy, but accelerated once more when this collapsed in 1978-79. Wage and price increases then moderated as unemployment rose, profits were squeezed and the exchange rate appreciated. From the middle of 1979, output fell.

To some extent, the rise in unemployment has been 'voluntary'. It has been due, that is, to more generous unemployment benefits in relation to earnings at work after tax, to changes in registration habits, and to some other such changes. However, a study by Nickell (1979) puts the effect of more generous unemployment benefits at no more than about a 0.2 points increase in the unemployment percentage, and Laslett (in Scott with Laslett, 1978, chapter 10) has estimated that the whole 'voluntary' increase has probably amounted to only about 1 point, thus lifting the average from 1.7 per cent in 1955-66 to 2.7 per cent of employees. Nevertheless, some take the view that the 'voluntary' increase has been appreciably more than this (see, e.g. Wood 1972), and one hears reports that, for example, London Transport cannot obtain workers to fill vacancies, and that seasonal workers in holiday resorts cannot be easily found.

In searching for other explanations of the rise in unemployment, one naturally turns to see what has happened to employment. Table 2 gives the main figures. Total numbers of employees in employment grew until 1966 and then fell. This is also what happened to male employment, but female employment grew (with some fluctuation) throughout the period, so that women now represent 41 per cent of all employees, as compared to only 32 per cent in 1950. It is the change in the industrial pattern of employment which explains most of this change in the sex-ratio. The male-determined industries (especially manufacturing, but also agriculture, mining, and the railways) have declined, whereas education, medical services, public administration and other services have expanded.

Since, for most of the period, an average woman employee only cost 0.65 times as much as an average male employee, the growth of numbers employed exaggerates the growth of male-equivalent employment. In Table 3, an attempt has been made to allow for this, and also for three other factors which have all tended in the same direction, that is, to make numbers employed grow faster than 'true' employment. These factors are : the decline in the length of the working week; the increase in holidays with pay; and the growth of part-time work. While the estimates are uncertain, they suggest that, since 1955, 'true' employment has probably grown about 1 per cent per annum more slowly than numbers employed. On this reckoning, total employment virtually stopped growing after 1955. However, these estimates do not alter the fact that the rate of decline in employment accelerated after 1966, just when unemployment started to rise.

North Sea Oil and Gas as a Cause of Unemployment

It has been suggested by some that the discovery and exploitation of oil and gas in the North Sea has been responsible for a substantial part of the rise in unemployment in the U.K. The argument seems to be as follows. Oil and gas from the North Sea have substituted for imported oil, or have been exported, and so have substantially improved the U.K.'s balance of payments on current account, thus tending to raise the value of the pound in terms of foreign currencies. The exchange rate has been further strengthened by an inflow of capital from OPEC countries and elsewhere which would have been much smaller had there been no prospect of oil and gas production. This strengthening of the exchange rate has reduced the competitiveness of U.K. export industries or those competing with imports, and especially of manufacturing industry. The result has been a decline in employment in those industries and a rise in unemployment.

One can put the argument in another way. North Sea oil and gas represent a big structural change in the U.K. economy. They compete most directly with traded goods industries, since they are essentially providers of foreign exchange. If resources were perfectly mobile, or if wages and prices were perfectly flexible, there would be no unemployment, but neither is the case. The structural change in the pattern of output required then leads to more unemployment since the non-traded goods industries do not absorb the redundant workers from the traded goods industries straight away. The decline in manufacturing is not smoothly and quickly offset by a expansion in other sectors of the economy, nor is the decline prevented by a sufficient fall in factor payments in manufacturing relative to those elsewhere. The effect of the capital inflow is similar. Ideally, investment in the U.K. should increase to match the inflow and the resulting worsening of the current account of the balance of payments. However, the capital is mostly invested in short-term deposits and investment does not increase. Instead, the worsening in the current account tends to reduce output, income and savings in the U.K., and unemployment rises.

There are three criticisms which may be made to this line of argument. First, in so far as North Sea oil and gas have increased real incomes in the U.K., or have provided extra resources via the capital inflow, they have reduced inflationary pressures (especially if real wage resistance is strong). They have therefore reduced the necessity for deflationary measures by the U.K. Government, and this has tended to increase employment and reduce unemployment. This point is further discussed in the next section. Secondly, putting that point aside and assuming that total output has been unaffected (apart from the 'pure gain' resulting from the rent element in North Sea oil and gas) the magnitude of North Sea oil and gas output (taking account of its related financing) has been too small to account for much of the fall in manufacturing output below trend. In the Appendix we estimate that less than a fifth of this fall can be attributed to oil and gas, and the effect of this on unemployment should have been largely offset by gains in employment in non-traded goods industries (including services). Thirdly, so far as capital inflows are concerned there have been other factors at work besides the prospect of oil and gas revenues. The U.K. Government has pursued a monetary policy leading to high interest rates which have, in turn, encouraged an inflow of capital. It has always been open to the Government to neutralise the effect of the capital inflow by purchases of foreign exchange for sterling[1], and the fact that it has chosen not to do so suggests that it has welcomed the high exchange rate as a factor assisting its deflationary policy. Without the oil, and with the same interest rates, the capital inflow might indeed have been smaller and the exchange rate lower. But then in order to achieve the same amount of deflation, the Government would have had to raise interest rates even further. So unemployment might have been much the same.

In conclusion, therefore, it seems that one cannot attribute much, if any, of the increase in unemployment in the U.K. to the North Sea oil and gas discoveries. As the next section shows, there are indeed some who would argue that unemployment has been reduced rather than increased as a result of them.

The Balance of Payments Constraint

The Cambridge Economic Policy Group (CEPG) have for some years, in their Reviews (1975-1980), put forward the view that it is the U.K.'s balance of payments which prevents successive Governments from pursuing more expansionary policies which would have led to faster growth in output and employment, to lower unemployment, and even to lower inflation as well. The crucial elements in their argument seem to have been as follows. The rate of growth of output for some years has been below the rate of growth of productive potential, because aggregate demand has not been allowed to increase fast enough. Had demand increased faster, output would have increased faster too, but this would have sucked in more imports and the balance of payments would have worsened. Since this worsening could not be tolerated, demand had to be restrained and unemployment allowed to grow. The slow growth of output has tended to aggravate inflation since fewer resources have become available to satisfy workers' aspirations. They have therefore pushed up money wage rates faster in an attempt to achieve certain real, post-tax wage targets which they have set themselves. The result has been to accentuate inflation, which growing unemployment has done little or nothing to prevent, since it has virtually no effect on either wage demands or customary profit margins.

If this view is accepted, it is clear that North Sea oil and gas, far from increasing unemployment, must have reduced it. By increasing the availability of foreign exchange they must have permitted a faster expansion of demand.

It might, at first blush, seem that the obvious remedy for this state of affairs would be to reflate demand and let the exchange rate depreciate. In fact, in 1972-3 this is precisely what was done, and output did expand and unemployment did fall – for a time. Unfortunately, inflation also accelerated, and so the policy was reversed. Inflation was brought down, but output fell and unemployment rose well above the levels of 1972.

The CEPG do not advocate reflation plus depreciation alone, precisely because they think it would lead to unacceptable rates of inflation, and require unacceptable rates of depreciation of the pound. Instead, they advocate reflation plus some depreciation, plus import restrictions through higher tariffs. They think this would not be inflationary rather the reverse. They claim that import restrictions would make more resources available to satisfy wage demands than would exchange rate depreciation, essentially for three reasons : (a) because the terms of trade would improve instead of worsening; (b) because profit margins would not be increased, whereas they would increase for exports with depreciation; and (c) because it would be possible to expand demand more quickly with import restrictions because the balance of payments would improve more quickly. They recognise that there would be a danger of retaliation against U.K. exports if U.K. tariffs on imports were increased, but they believe that this could be avoided if other countries could be brought to realise that the restrictions were benefitting the U.K. without harming them, since total imports would not be reduced.

Arguments against the CEPG's framework of thought and

against their policy recommendations have been set out elsewhere (see Scott, Little and Corden, 1980, and Allsopp and Joshi, 1980). The main points are as follows. First, and most importantly, it is not fear of worsening the balance of payments but fear of inflation which has prevented successive Governments from expanding demand faster. The CEPG's own analysis of the arguments against reflation plus exchange rate depreciation point to this conclusion, and the experience of 1972-3 has provided a lesson which has not yet been forgotten. Secondly, there is no good reason to believe that import restrictions would be less inflationary than exchange rate depreciation. Neither points (b) nor (c) in the preceding paragraph carry weight, and while point (a) seems valid, it also provides a valid reason why foreign countries should retaliate against U.K. exports, in addition to other reasons. The U.K. would, if it increased its tariffs substantially and by increasing amounts over a period of at least a decade (and this is what is envisaged), not only be in breach of its international agreements, but also be injuring particular exporters from particular countries, who would regard the possible benefits to other exporters elsewhere as irrelevant. Furthermore, the CEPC ignore the adverse effects on efficiency of high and increasing tariffs, as well as the effects on wages push of a strenghtening of monopolistic elements in the U.K.

Labour-Using versus Labour-Saving Investment

In the immediate post-war years, profits were high, but since then their share in industrial and commercial, but excluding oil, companies' value-added (i.e. the sum of gross trading profits and incomes from employment earned and paid by companies) has steadily fallen. This fall could normally have been expected to reduce the ratio of investment to companies' value-added. However, for a variety of reasons, including more preferential tax treatment, companies have increased the ratio of investment to gross trading profits quite substantially. As a result, the ratio of investment to value-added actually rose until about 1966, and did not fall appreciably until after 1973. However, the falling share of profits in value-added may have changed the character of the investment undertaken so that it became less labour-using and more labour-saving. This would then have resulted in a relatively slower growth of employment opportunities, and would help to explain the slowing down in the growth of employment shown in Tables 2 and 3.

Some reasons for thinking that a fall in the share of profits would have this kind of effect are given in Scott with Laslett, 1978, Chapter 5, and I hope to develop these in a forthcoming book on economic growth. A fall in the share of profits implies a rise in that of wages which, in turn, implies that the real product wage has risen faster than average labour productivity. In that sense, labour has become relatively more expensive. Some may feel that it is indeed likely that businessmen will then select more projects which save labour (and increase output less) at the expense of projects which increase both employment and output. Provided total investment is unaffected, a change of its composition in this direction, towards labour-saving, should lead to a faster growth in productivity. It should also slow down the growth of both output capacity and employment. Up to 1973, there is some evidence in the U.K. for both effects.

Table 4 contrasts the experience of the manufacturing and 'private service' groups of industries in the U.K. Whereas the share of profits fell over the whole period in manufacturing, there is no strong downward trend in private services. As may be seen from Table 2, employment in manufacturing fell after 1966, whereas employment in private services rose throughout the period. In the latter case, the rise was probably helped by the marked increase in the ratio of investment to value-added which occurred, as well as by the fact that the share of profits in value-added did not fall so much.

No figures are given here of output and productivity, but there does seem to have been some acceleration in the rate of growth of productivity in manufacturing up to 1973, especially if allowance is made for falling hours per worker as in Table 3. Furthermore, the growth of capacity output appears to have slowed down (see Scott with Laslett, 1978, p. 62). On the other hand, experience since 1973 is difficult to reconcile with the hypothesis. As in many countries, there has been a marked slowing down in the rate of growth of productivity in manufacturing. For these years, it seems as if there may have been labour hoarding, or at any rate a reluctance to dismiss workers very fast (and incur the resulting redundancy expenditures). Alternatively, or as well, some investment may have been simply wasted, since it was undertaken on incorrect expectations about the rate of growth of the economy. Steel is an obvious example. If this could be deducted, the rate of 'useful' investment might appear much lower than the figures suggest, and this could help to explain the poor productivity performance.

It still has to be explained why the share of profits should have fallen. To some extent this may have resulted from a failure by companies to adjust their accounts for inflation. They may have fixed their prices and profit margins in the light of their historic, rather than current, costs (see Table 8 and the further discussion in the next Section). Apart from that, the main explanation probably was that successive governments pursued deflationary policies which squeezed profit margins, or, when conditions were favourable for price increases, prevented these by means of controls. The next section discusses these policies.

The Policies of Governments from 1964 to 1974

There is not space here to review properly the ways in which the policies of successive Governments affected employment and unemployment. Only fiscal and monetary policies and incomes policies will be considered and very briefly at that. The account which follows draws heavily on Blackaby (1978) for the period up to 1974, and on Davies (1979) for 1974-79. Tables 5, 6 and 7 provide some relevant statistics for the period since the middle 1960's, which is when unemployment started to increase and the growth in employment decelerated markedly.

In October 1964, the incoming Labour Government confronted a severe balance of payments crisis, resulting in part from the expansionary policies of its predecessor. The Government had intended to abolish 'stop-go' and accelerate the rate of growth of the economy, and a National Plan setting out its objectives was published about a year after taking office. However, the initial decision was taken that the pound should not be devalued, and policy was dominated by the need to defend the exchange rate in a succession of crises whose immediate causes were speculative capital movements. As may be seen from Table 7, Bank Rate was raised, lowered, raised again and lowered again, and then raised once more before devaluation finally was accepted in November 1967. The accompanying fiscal and monetary policies were not especially restrictive (Tables 5 and 6), but it became clearer and clearer that growth could not proceed according to the Plan. In 1967 unemployment rose above 2 per cent, then considered to be high, and this was one of the factors which finally induced the Government to accept devaluation. Nevertheless, that did not provide the occasion for more expansionary policies. On the contrary, in order to provide 'room' for the required improvement in the balance of payments, public expenditure, which had been growing rapidly in real terms, was decisively cut back. The 1968 budget was one of the most deflationary ones since the War, and this deflationary trend was continued in 1969, when, at last, the balance of payments showed clear signs of improvement.

For the devaluation to be successful, as was widely recognised, domestic prices and wages had to be held in check. Unfortunately, this became increasingly difficult to ensure. Soon after taking office, the Labour Government had secured a voluntary agreement (the 'Statement of Intent') with unions and employers to keep wage and price increases under review. This was followed by the setting up of formal administrative machinery, the National Board for Prices and Incomes, to undertake the review. A 'norm' of 3 to 3.5 per cent for wage increases was agreed in 1965. However, the rate of wage increases accelerated to well above this norm, and so steps were taken to tighten up the 'review' which appeared to have no effect. Finally, following the seamen's strike in May 1966 which touched off a serious run on the pound, the Government introduced a statutory 6 months freeze on wages, salaries, dividends and prices, which was followed by a further 6 months of severe restraint, with a nil norm, but with exceptions for productivity increases. These measures succeeded in checking wage increases, but they were accepted only with reluctance by the trades unions. The period of severe restraint ended a few months before the devaluation, which therefore came just when the loyalty and patience of the unions was beginning to become exhausted. After a period of some relaxation, when wage increases accelerated, the Government attempted to tighten up the policy again. However, the exceptions allowed for productivity increases became increasingly exploited and, perhaps partly influenced by the increased militancy of students and unions all over the world, wage increases finally 'exploded' in 1969-70 in the run-up to the election, when the Government abandoned all effective attempts to restrain them along with its legislative attempts to reform industrial relations.
Meanwhile, unemployment had been slowly creeping up, not surprisingly in view of the restrictive fiscal and monetary policies pursued in 1969-70. The Conservative Government which took office in June 1970 did not, however, feel able to counteract this immediately by strong reflationary measures in view of the wage explosion, which was leading to a price

explosion. The Government was in principle opposed to intervention in wage bargaining, and the NBPI was wound up. However, it was inevitably involved in public sector wage settlements, where it had, initially, some success in moderating them. The growth of unemployment became faster in 1971, and the Government's policies became increasingly dominated by this. Both fiscal and monetary measures were used to expand demand, but, as usual, the effects on employment were lagged, and unemployment reaced a post-war peak of close to one million in the first quarter of 1972, when the situation was aggravated by a coal miners' strike which led to a three-day working week. The strike was finally settled on favourable terms to the miners.

These events led to the so-called U-turn in Government policy. Non-intervention and rising unemployment had failed to moderate wage increases : so intervention and expansionary measures to reduce unemployment became the order of the day. The expansion was secured by both fiscal and monetary policies, and superimposed on an already rather expansionary situation, which the lag in unemployment had concealed. The result was that unemployment was brought sharply down, unfilled vacancies came sharply up, and the economy was caught off balance by three further inflationary shocks. First, the balance of payments, not surprisingly, went rapidly into deficit, and this was met by allowing the pound to float downwards from June 1972. Secondly, the pressure on import prices was increased by the world boom in commodity prices which got under way in the Autumn of 1972. Thirdly, there was the enormous increase in oil prices towards the end of 1973. Against these inflationary forces the Government set a statutory prices and incomes policy, starting with a short freeze at the end of 1972, which was succeeded by. Stages II and III and a Pay Board and Price Commission. While these almost certainly moderated wage increases, the latter were nevertheless substantial, and Stage III, which started in November 1973, was rather quickly destroyed by a second miners' strike and the defeat of Conservative Government at the resulting general election in February 1974.

Once again the incoming Labour Government was confronted with a serious balance of payments deficit and an underlying inflationary situation, only this time both were much worse. Somewhat recklessly, the preceding Government's price and incomes policy was abandoned and replaced by a voluntary 'social contract' with the unions which, effectively, placed no restraints at all on wage increases. The one element in the preceding policy which was retained proved to be highly inflationary. This was the 'threshold agreements' which provided an automatic link between increases in the cost of living and wages. The result was a pay and prices explosion which was the worst so far experienced, wage increases exceeding, and price increases nearly reaching, 25 per cent. The Government started in 1974 by relaxing both fiscal and monetary policies, thus adding to the inflationary pressures. Nonetheless, output was falling and unemployment started to grow again, soon quite rapidly to levels not reached since before the war.

There were, in fact, some powerful deflationary factors at work. The ratio of personal savings as conventionally measured to personal disposable income was 9.5 per cent in 1972, but rose to 14.0 per cent in 1975, and real consumers' expenditure fell in both 1974 and 1975. Company profits, net of stock appreciation and capital consumption at replacement cost, fell drastically, so that pre-tax real rates of return in 1974 and 1975 were around half their levels in the 1960's (Table 8). Prices on the stock exchange plunged to very low levels, and some financial and property companies were bankrupted. A more serious crisis was averted by the 'lifeboat' provided by the Bank of England and other banks. Not surprisingly, gross fixed investment fell, but the biggest turnround was in stockbuilding, which was strongly negative in 1975.

To a large extent, it seems to have been the rapid inflation itself which was deflating the economy. There is a tremendous difference between the accounts of the different sectors of the economy adjusted for inflation and unadjusted (see Table 9). The personal sector lost heavily as it was the chief holder of assets denominated in terms of money, whose real value was thus being rapidly eroded by inflation. The chief gainer from this was the public sector. If one allows for these losses and gains, it appears that the public sector, far from having a financial deficit, had a large surplus. It seems quite likely that it was this which led to the fall in consumption and rise in personal savings ratio as conventionally measured. Consumers were aware of their real losses of wealth, and struggled to rebuild their stocks of monetary assets. So far as companies are concerned, since they, on balance, held net monetary liabilities, their positions were in this respect strengthened by the faster inflation. However, this was swamped by the fact that price increases lagged behind cost increases. On a historic cost basis their profits looked reasonable (Table 8), but these profits did not allow

sufficiently for the rapidly rising cost of inputs. Hence
companies were subjected to a severe liquidity squeeze (Table
9).

It might have been expected that a Labour Government,
faced with these deflationary tendencies, would have reflated
the economy, at least enough to prevent unemployment increasing
from levels which, in 1974, still looked high by the standards
of the 1950's or 1960's. Indeed, in his November 1974 Budget,
the Chancellor said that he would 'ensure that the rise in
unemployment will be modest in 1975, and that its level will
remain well below 1 million'. He added : 'to adopt deliberately
a strategy which requires mass unemployment would be no less
uneconomic than a moral crime.

There is no real evidence that the adoption of
deflationary policies will produce a worthwhile impact on the
rate of inflation. To throw a million people out of work would
be like burning down the Houses of Parliament to roast a
chicken'.

Nevertheless, as Tables 5, 6 and 7 show, the Government's
fiscal policy in the next three years was deflationary, the
money supply was held back and interest rates were allowed to
rise to unprecedented levels. Furthermore, unemployment grew
rapidly, exceeding one million comfortably by the end of 1975
and remaining at over 1.25 million for the rest of the
Government's period of office (i.e. until May 1979). The
weakness of the balance of payments and the depreciation of the
pound accompanying it forced the Government to apply to the
International Monetary Fund for assistance in 1976. By then,
however, the Prime Minister seems to have become convinced that
Keynesian remedies for unemployment no longer worked, and that
unemployment was due to excessive wage increases[2].

The combination of rapid inflation and a foreign exchange
crisis with rising unemployment was enough to induce trade
union leaders to cooperate with the Government in a very tough
incomes policy. By means of real wage cuts in two successive
years, 1976 and 1977, the rate of inflation was brought down to
single figures in 1978 (Table 1). This reduction in wage and
price inflation reversed some of the deflationary forces
mentioned above and for this, and other reasons the economy
staged a modest recovery (although unemployment remained high).
As so often before, it then proved impossible to maintain the
incomes policy. Wages accelerated and the Government was

involved in a series of confrontations with unions in the
public sector especially. The 'winter of discontent' of 1978-9
contributed to the defeat of the Labour Party at the election
of May 1979.

Some Lessons

Three successive Governments under the compulsion of
events have felt it necessary to abandon policies they had
intended to pursue. The two Labour Governments of 1964 and 1974
intended to expand the economy, but ended up deflating it. The
first watched unemployment rise from 354 thousand[3] in the last
quarter of 1964 to 598 thousand in the second quarter of 1970.
The second saw it rise from 575 thousand in the first quarter
of 1974 to 1,304 thousand in the second quarter of 1979. The
Conservative Government of 1970 was going to reduce inflation
'at a stroke' without intervention in wage bargaining. In fact,
worried by the increase in unemployment from 598 thousand
(second quarter of 1970) to 910 thousand (first quarter of
1972), which appeared to have no impact on wages and prices,
they inflated the economy and tried to hold prices and wages in
check by means of controls. Prices had risen by 6 per cent
over the year ending in the second quarter of 1970, when they
took office. They rose by 13 per cent over the year ending in
the first quarter of 1974, when they left it.

It is tempting to conclude from this sorry record that
British Governments are unable to control either unemployment
or inflation. They have to let unemployment increase if the
alternative is either a foreign exchange crisis (as in the
1960's and, to some extent, in 1975-6) or high inflation (as in
1975-6). They have to let inflation increase if the alternative
is a high level of unemployment (as in 1972). What is to be
regarded as 'high' depends on the apparent alternative. The
higher is inflation, the higher is the unemployment which the
electorate will tolerate, and vice-versa.

An explanation for what has happened in the U.K. then runs
along the following lines (see especially Phelps Brown, 1975).
Wages in the U.K. are settled mainly through collective
bargaining, not (as in the Scandinavian countries or at times
in the Netherlands) in one of a very few bargains covering all
or most of the economy, but through a fairly decentralized and
complex system of what might be called fragmented labour
monopolies. Each monopoly has some power, but is uncertain

just how much. Each will push for the maximum wage it thinks
it 'safe' to obtain, but what is 'safe'? After the war, the
labour force was dominated by those with memories of the hard
inter-war years. The post-war world looked much better, and
they achieved much bigger money and also real wage increases.
But they remained cautious because of their experience between
the wars. Eventually, under the warm sun of full employment,
and exasperated by the restraint they were put under by the
Labour Government of 1964-70, and finally, with the example of
the militant students and labour of other countires in 1968,
they pushed really hard in 1969-70, and there was the first pay
explosion and a big increase in days of work lost through
strikes. Since then, militancy may have further increased.
What this means is that now, in the absence of an effective
incomes policy (on which see below), as compared with the
1950's or 1960's, more unemployment and/or bigger threat of
bankruptcies is needed to prevent wages accelerating, and still
more to make them decelerate. In monetarist terms, the natural
level of unemployment has increased, although monetarists would
not, in general, accept the above account of why this has
happened.
    Since the electorate dislikes both inflation and un-
employment, Governments try to avoid both. But the forces
described in the preceding paragraph have compelled governments
to accept more of both. Why both? A monetarist would argue
that a rise in the natural level of unemployment need not lead
to more inflation, although it is bound to increase
unemployment in the end. The reason both go together is that,
before the elctorate will accept a higher level of
unemployment, it has to be convinced that the alternative is
higher inflation and, to convince the electorate of that,
higher inflation needs to be experienced. In principle,
inflation could be brought down to zero and unemployment left
at its natural level, but would the electorate be content if
that level seemed historically high? In order to convince the
electorate that a high level of unemployment has to be
tolerated, inflation may actually have to be high - that, at
least, seems to be the lesson of previous years.

    In principle, it should be possible for everyone to accept
much lower nominal wage increases without that affecting their
real wage increases. Inflation could then be reduced, and
unemployment as well. This has always been the main aim of
prices and incomes policies. But the experience we have
reviewed suggests that, at least in the U.K., incomes policies
of the rather wide variety which have been tried do not work
for more than a couple of years. There are several reasons for

this, but perhaps the fundamental one is that the loyalty and patience of workers and their leaders is eventually exhausted. In a crisis, they are prepared to forgo their power to extract large (nominal) wage increases through bargaining, but they are not prepared to forgo it once the crisis seems past. Usually, when that happens, they try to make up for lost ground, and there is a wage explosion, as happened in 1969-70, in 1974-5, and in 1978-80. This seems to be another lesson.

Present Government Policies

The present Conservative Government took office in May 1979 with some intentions similar to those of its predecessor in 1970. It wanted to reduce government intervention, especially in wage-bargaining. It also intended to bring down the rate of inflation, then accelerating. For this purpose, it relied mainly on control of the money supply. Interest rates were quickly raised, with the Bank of England's Minimum Lending Rate reaching an unprecedented 17 per cent per annum on 15 November 1979. Despite much faster inflation in the U.K. than in other OECD countries, the exchange rate appreciated. Competitiveness, measured by unit labour costs relative to those of competitor countries, deteriorated by about 30 per cent in the year ending in the first quarter of 1980 (see the Treasury index referred to in The Financial Times, 14 July 1980). The result has been declining profitability, especially in manufacturing industry, increased bankruptcies, rising unemployment, and falling output.

In the wage-round ending around mid 1980 there was not much sign that wage increases on average were much affected by the recession. The preceding Labour Government had, in effect, left a number of post-dated cheques in the form of large public sector wage increases which took effect in 1979-80. Some private sector wage increases were well below the increase in the cost of living - where bankruptcies or shut-downs threatened. The steel strike was settled on terms which could hardly be regarded as favourable to the steel workers. Nevertheless, on average, wages increased faster in nominal terms than in the previous year, and the rate of increase in retail prices also accelerated, thanks partly to the shift from direct to indirect taxation in the June 1979 Budget.

However, there was a slow-down in wage and price increases in the succeeding wage round. Had this not occurred, the position would have been very serious. It is serious enough as it is since, although a sufficient slow-down will eventually

permit expansion to be resumed, the question which remains
unanswered is what the level of unemployment will need to be to
keep wages in check. It is important to remember that there are
at present two forces, which must be carefully distinguished,
which are moderating wage increases. First, there is the high
level of unemployment. Secondly, there is the threat of shutdown and bankruptcy. The second of these cannot persist if
growth is to be resumed. For that to occur, the private sector
must be earning reasonable profits, and sufficient to make it
invest enough in total, and enough in the labour-using
direction, to absorb the growing labour force. At some point,
therefore, if unemployment is to stop growing, profits and
investment must rise and the threat of bankruptcy and shutdown
be removed, at least for most firms. When that happens, only
one of the above two restraints on wages will remain :
unemployment.

Some monetarists take the view that unemployment will not
have to be high or, at any rate, no higher than people
voluntarily wish it to be. Once inflationary expectations are
broken, why should workers price themselves out of the market
by demanding excessive wage increases? This view of the matter
seems to neglect the monopolistic situation in which collective
bargaining occurs. Each group may have considerable unexploited
bargaining strength, especially in the short run. The attempt
by each to exploit this, however, leads to a general increase
in wages all round, since a few key settlements can affect
expectations, and lead to comparisons being made which both
employers and workers accept as relevant. The electricity
workers for example, could secure a much higher relative wage
in the long run if other workers were unorganised. But they
are not. Unemployment, and/or the threat of shut down, has
then to be sufficient to deter the electricity workers and
others like them from demanding large nominal wage increases.
The system could cope with one or a very few, labour monopolies
(or with none!), but not with the large number we have. There
are too many well-organised groups whose ability to disrupt the
economy is so great that it generally appears attractive to buy
them off with a large nominal wage increase.

It is, however, over-simplified to regard unemployment and
bankruptcies as the only factors which keep wages in check. The
electricity workers might not wish to exploit their monopoly
position to the full even if there were full employment and

prosperity. Public opinion and the support, or lack of it, which they get from other unions, must exert a considerable influence over many workers. A strike over an 'unreasonable' pay demand will not receive sufficient support to last very long.

The need is, then, to create sufficient understanding and backing for a system of wage-fixing which will give most workers only moderate nominal wage increases when unemployment is low and profits are sufficiently high (Blackaby, 1980). They must be induced to feel that moderate increases in these circumstances are 'reasonable', and must withdraw their support from those who want to press for bigger wage increases, despite the fact that these increases could be secured by threat of strike. They must do so, perhaps, because they realise that this is the best way to make the system work, and that, over a long period, it will deliver them more than alternative systems. One has the impression that in some other countries, such as Austria, West Germany and Switzerland, this understanding and backing exists, but it seems to be lacking in the U.K. The explanation may lie in history, and perhaps only experience teaches.

There is an issue which has to be confronted. If money wage increases are not moderated, employment must suffer in the long run. Inflation is an evasion of this issue, since it appears to give high wage increases without reducing employment. But the high wage increases are mostly a sham, and the pretence can only continue as long as inflation accelerates, which it cannot be allowed to do indefinitely. At some point the Government must call a halt, and that indeed is what the present Government is trying to do.

The policy has many critics, since its effects on unemployment and output are so manifestly bad, and since its effects on inflation are slow to appear. But if a halt is to be called at some point, it is hard to see that postponement will make the process any less painful. On the contrary, the longer inflationary expectations are allowed to persist, the harder will they eventually be to eradicate. The present time, when there is still a lot of North Sea oil and gas to come, is a better one to grasp the nettle.

The main justification for the policy is that it does confront everyone with the real issue between wage increases and employment. One hopes it will make everyone readier to seek and accept a long-lasting solution. Thus far, that solution is not yet in sight.

Notes

1] This is controversial. Some would argue that the Government cannot achieve a given monetary target and simultaneously prevent the exchange rate from appreciating if the resulting combination of interest rates and exchange rate are such as to induce an inflow of capital from abroad. It is certainly true that the U.K. Government abandoned the attempt to hold down the exchange rate in 1977 in just this sort of situation. In principle, however, there would seem to be no limit to the Government's ability to buy foreign exchange for sterling, and to neutralise the effects on the money supply by suitable open market sales of securities. The difficulty may be that if, in the end, the exchange rate is allowed to appreciate, the Government will make a large loss on its transactions, since the foreign exchange it has accumulated will be worth less than the sterling liabilities incurred to pay for it.

2] See the report of the Prime Minister, Mr. Callaghan's speech to the Labour Party Conference in The Times, 29 September 1976.

3] All unemployment figures refer to the U.K., exclude school-leavers and students, and are seasonally adjusted.

Table 1

Unemployment, Inflation and Growth of Output in the U.K.

Years	Percentage(a) unemployed (1)	Rate of increase of retail prices (2)	Rate of increase of earnings (3)	Per cent per annum Rate of increase of real earnings (4)	Rate of growth of real GDP (5)
1950–55	1.4	5.5	8.3	2.6	2.8
1955–60	1.7	2.7	5.4	2.6	2.4
1960–66	1.7	3.6	5.9	2.2	2.9
1966–67	2.3	2.4	3.1	0.7	2.2
1967–68	2.5	4.8	8.2	3.2	4.4
1968–69	2.4	5.4	7.8	2.3	2.4
1969–70	2.6	6.4	12.0	5.4	2.0
1970–71	3.4	9.4	11.4	1.8	1.5
1971–72	3.7	7.1	12.9	5.3	2.6
1972–73	2.6	9.2	13.2	3.7	7.2
1973–74	2.6	16.1	17.7	1.5	-1.8
1974–75	3.9	24.2	26.7	2.0	-1.1
1975–76	5.3	16.5	15.7	-0.7	2.7
1976–77	5.7	15.8	9.0	-5.9	1.9
1977–78	5.7	8.3	13.0	4.3	3.2
1978–79	5.4	13.4	15.5	1.9	1.6
1979–80	6.8	18.0	20.7	2.3	-2.0

(a) Refers to later of pair of years, or average of all except first of years shown.

Notes to Table 1
(1) Unemployed, excl. school leavers, average for year, as percentage of itself plus employees in employment at June. Economic Trends
(2) Index of retail prices. Economic Trends.
(3) 1950 to 1963, average of April and October figures for average weekly earnings of manual male workers, 21 or over, in manufacturing and certain other industries, from Britain Labour Statistics Historical Abstracts, pp. 103, 108 linking at Oct. 1959. 1963-1976, all workers in production industries and some services, 'older series'; and 1976-79 'new series' covering whole economy, Economic Trends.
(4) Col (3) deflated by col (2)
(5) GDP at constant factor cost, average of expenditure, income and output estimates. Economic Trends.

Table 2
Employees in Employment in the U.K. 1950-78

Industry				Millions at mid-year		
	1950	1955	1960	1966	1973	1978
1. Agriculture etc.	0.98	0.84	0.74	0.58	0.43	0.38
2. Manufacturing	7.54	8.16	8.42	8.58	7.83	7.23
3. 'Public industry'	2.97	2.94	2.79	2.62	2.23	2.16
4. Construction	1.31	1.37	1.43	1.65	1.38	1.26
5. Distribution	2.22	2.47	2.74	2.92	2.74	2.76
6. 'Private Services'	2.22	2.29	2.45	2.89	3.21	3.57
7. 'Public Services'	2.90	3.03	3.33	4.01	4.83	5.29
8. Total	20.05	21.05	21.89	23.25	22.66	22.67
of which males	13.55	13.92	14.31	14.84	13.77	13.33
females	6.50	7.13	7.58	8.41	8.89	9.33

	Rates of growth, % p.a., between years shown.				
	1950-55	1955-60	1960-66	1966-73	1973-78
9. Agriculture etc.	-3.0	-2.5	-1.2	-4.1	-2.4
10. Manufacturing	1.6	0.6	0.3	-1.3	-1.6
11. 'Public industry'	-0.,2	-1.0	-1.0	-2.3	-0.7
12. Construction	0.9	0.8	2.4	-2.5	-1.7
13. Distribution	2.2	2.1	1.1	-0.9	0.1
14. 'Private Services'	0.6	1.3	2.8	1.5	2.2
15. 'Public Services'	0.9	1.9	3.2	2.7	1.8
16. Total	1.0	0.8	1.0	-0.4	0.0
Males	0.5	0.6	0.6	-1.1	-0.6
Females	1.9	1.2	1.7	0.8	1.0

Notes to Table 2

'Public industry'	= mining and quarrying, gas, electricity and water, transport and communication, most of which is nationalized.
'Private services'	= insurance, banking, finance and business services and miscellaneous services. Private domestic servants are excluded.
'Public services'	= educational, modical and dental and other professional and scientific services, public administration and defence, but excluding H.M. Forces.

The totals exclude self-employed, private domestic servants and H.M. Forces. They may not exactly equal the sums of the components, partly because of rounding and a small unallocated category of workers, and partly because, before 1960, they were linked on separately from the components.

Source
See Scott with Laslett, 1978, Table 5.2.

Table 3

Numbers at Work and Man-Hours Worked, U.K. 1950-78

	1950	1955	1960	1966	1973	1978
1. Employees in employment (millions)	20.05	21.05	21.89	23.25	22.66	22.66
2. Equivalent male man-hours p.a. (thous. millions)	37.57	39.68	39.86	39.42	36.17	34.89
3. Ditto per employee (hours p.a.)	1874	1885	1820	1695	1596	1539

Rates of increase, per cent per annum

	1950-55	1955-60	1960-66	1966-73	1973-78
4. Employees in employment	1.0	0.8	1.0	-0.4	0.0
5. Equivalent male man-hours p.a.	1.1	0.1	-0.2	-1.2	-0.7
6. Ditto per employee	0.1	-0.7	-1.2	-0.9	-0.7

Notes to Table 3
Number of employees in employment as in Table 2. Equivalent male man-hours allows for estimated changes in hours per working week, number of weeks holidays per annum, number of part-time workers, and number of women workers. A part-time worker is counted as one half of a full-time worker, and a woman full-time worker as 0.65 of a male full-time worker (based on earnings ratios). Estimates are less precise than the figures given may suggest.

Sources : New Earnings Surveys, Department of Employment Gazette and British Labour Statistics Yearbooks and Historical Abstract.

Table 4

Shares of Profits and Investments in Value-Added

	Percentages				
	1951–55	1965–60	1961–66	1967–73	1974–78
Profits/value added					
Manufacturing	34.9	32.1	29.8	27.1	20.2
'Private Services'	38.7	39.8	35.4	36.4	36.1
Investment/value added					
Manufacturing	15.4	15.5	15.7	14.6	15.0
"Private Services'	5.5	7.4	9.9	11.7	12.2

Notes to Table 4
Both profits and value-added exclude stock appreciation, but depreciation (or capital consumption) has not been deducted. Some small amounts of income from self-employment are included in manufacturing profits, and they are probably a larger part of 'private services' profits. Value added is the sum of profits, thus defined, and income from employment. 'Private Services' are defined more or less in Table 2, but private domestic services is included in income from employment. While the attempt has been made to provide continuous series, the resulting estimates are uncertain, particularly for the earlier years for private services.

Source :
As for Table 5.3 in Scott with Laslett, 1978, but the figures for 1970 onwards allow for recent substantial revisions which have been made to the official estimates of profits.

Table 5

Changes in Fiscal Stance, 1963/4 to 1979/80

Fiscal years April-March	Percentage of 'high employment' GDP : changes from previous year in weighted balance of the public sector.
1963/4	-1.8
1964/5	-0.1
1965/6	1.5
1966/7	-0.1
1967/8	-0.4
1968/9	2.8
1969/70	2.7
1970/1	-0.9
1971/2	-1.1
1972/3	-1.6
1973/4	-1.1
1974/5	-1.1
1975/6	1.4
1976/7	1.3
1977/8	1.9
1978/9	0.0
1979/80	1.2

Note

The figures are a measure of discretionary changes in fiscal policy. They show the changes in the public sector (central and local government and public corporations) financial net surplus (broadly, current surplus less gross investment plus net capital transfer and tax receipts) over the previous year which would have occurred if GDP had been at a 'high employment' level in both years but tax rates and public sector expenditure had changed as they did. However, both receipts and expenditures are weighted (multiplied by positive numbers less than one) on the assumption that their 'first round' effects on domestic output are less than the nominal amounts because of 'leaks' to private savings and imports. The change in the weighted surplus is then expressed as a percentage of 'high employment' GDP. A positive figure in the table thus indicates that fiscal policy has become more deflationary. The estimates from 1963/4 to 1973/4 are from R.W.R. Price, 'Budgetary Policy', Table 4.9, p. 187 in Blackaby (ed), 1978. For later years they are from National Institute Economic Review, May 1980, p. 21.

Table 6

Measures of Monetary Tightness

Year   Percentage deviation of money stock, at mid-year,
           from trend ratio of stock to total final expenditure.

	Stock M1	Stock £M 3
1963	-2.2	-3.0
4	-0.8	-3.5
5	0.0	-1.8
6	1.3	0.1
7	0.1	-0.3
8	1.0	0.6
9	-2.1	-1.3
1970	-0.4	-3.2
1	3.1	-2.3
2	9.6	8.3
3	7.7	13.9
4	-6.6	14.3
5	-7.0	4.7
6	-7.1	-4.2
7	-6.0	-8.2

Note
The two money stocks are as defined in the Bank of England
Quarterly Bulletin, June 1980, and breaks in the continuity of
the series have been adjusted (so as to obtain as continuous a
series as possible) by the Bank of England, who kindly provided
the adjusted series. Broadly speaking, M1 consists of notes and
coin in circulation with the public plus sterling sight
deposits held by the U.K. private sector, while sterling M3
includes M1 plus all other sterling deposits (including
certificates of deposit) held by U.K. residents in both the
public and private sectors. Total final expenditure is the sum
of consumers' expenditure, general government final
consumption, gross domestic investment and exports of goods and
services. An exponential trend was fitted to the ratios of
stock : expenditure, and the table shows percentage deviations
from this. A minus sign indicates greater monetary tightness.
As may be seen, there is a certain ambiguity in the measure.

Table 7

Turning Points in Bank Rate or Minimum Lending Rate

Date at which lowest rate was increased, or highest rate was decreased	Rate, % p.a., at	
	low point	high point
27 Feb. 1964	4	
3 June 1965		7
14 July 1966	6	
26 Jan. 1967		7
19 Oct 1967	5.5	
21 March 1968		8
27 Feb. 1969	7	
5 March 1970		8
22 June 1972	5	
19 Jan. 1973		9
20 July 1973	7.5	
4 Jan. 1974		13
2 May. 1975	9.75	
14 Nov. 1975		12
23 Apr. 1976	9.25	
19 Nov. 1977		15
25 Nov. 1976	5	
28 Feb. 1979		14
12 June 1979	12	
3 July 1980		17

Sources :
Annual Abstracts of Statistics and National Institute Economic
Reviews. Minor fluctuations in April 1973 and in January 1978
have been omitted.

Table 8

Rates of Return on Trading Assets of Industrial and Commercial Companies (excl. North Sea activities).

Per cent per annum

	Pre-tax historical cost	Pre-tax real	Post-tax real
1963	16.1	11.6	6.5
1964	16.9	12.1	6.8
1965	16.0	11.4	6.3
1966	14.3	10.1	4.3
1967	13.7	10.2	4.6
1968	15.0	10.3	5.0
1969	15.0	10.0	5.2
1970	14.5	8.7	4.4
1971	15.3	8.9	5.1
1972	16.8	9.3	4.9
1973	19.6	8.8	6.1
1974	19.1	5.2	4.3
1975	17.7	4.7	3.6
1976	19.6	5.1	3.8
1977	18.8	5.8	4.2
1978	18.0	5.9	4.5
1979	17.8	4.1	3.5

Note

The real pre-tax return differs from the historic cost one by using capital consumption based on current replacement cost instead of the book value of depreciation, and by adjusting for stock appreciation. For further details see the source, Bank of England Quarterly Bulletin, June 1980, p. 191, and the references there given.

Table 9

Inflation Adjustments for Loss or Gain on Net Monetary Assets

Net acquisition of financial assets £ thousand millions

	1972	1973	1974	1975	1976	1977	1978
Personal sector							
1. Unadjusted	1.5	2.8	5.0	6.9	7.9	8.0	9.8
2. Loss on real value of net monetary assets	−3.2	−4.7	−10.7	−13.9	−8.7	−8.7	−6.1
3. Adjusted (1+2)	−1.7	−1.9	−5.7	−7.0	−0.8	−0.7	3.7
Public sector							
4. Unadjusted	−1.6	−2.7	−4.8	−7.9	−8.3	−5.7	−7.2
5. Gain on real value of net monetary liabilities	3.2	4.3	9.4	13.0	8.2	9.5	6.6
6. Adjusted (4+5)	1.6	1.6	4.6	5.1	−0.1	3.8	−0.6
Company sector							
7. Unadjusted	0.5	−1.7	−5.1	−1.4	−1.8	−3.0	−3.5
8. Gain on real value of net monetary liabilities	0.2	0.3	1.2	1.4	0.3	0.5	0.1
9. Adjusted (7+8)	0.7	−1.4	−3.9	−0.1	−1.4	−2.5	−3.4

Note

'Net acquisition of financial assets' = gross savings less gross investment plus net capital transfer receipts. The loss or gain on net monetary assets has been estimated by multiplying the estimated nominal value of assets denominated in money terms, less similar liabilities, at mid-year by the proportionate increase in the price index of consumers' expenditure over the year (fourth quarter of preceding year to fourth quarter of year in question). However, assets denominated in foreign currencies were also multiplied by the change in the relevant exchange rate. For further details, see the source used, which was Taylor and Threadgold, 1979.

Appendix : The Effect of North Sea Oil and Gas on Manufacturing Output

In this Appendix we make a crude estimate of the effect of North Sea oil and gas on manufacturing output in 1980 and relate it to the fall in output below trend which has occurred. We assume throughout that the aggregate level of outpup, excluding what we call the 'pure gain' from the North Sea, has not been affected by the oil and gas discoveries. This, for reasons discussed in the text, almost certainly exaggerates our estimate of the fall in manufacturing output due to oil and gas. Indeed, it is quite possible to argue that the net effect, taking everything into account, has been to raise rather than reduce manufacturing output. However, if we make the assumption of unchanged aggregate output, we conclude that, at most, about 37 per cent of the fall in manufacturing below trend could be attributed to the oil and gas. For a number of reasons, however, this greatly exaggerates the fall, and it seems likely that the actual fall, on the assumption mentioned, due to oil and gas was less than one quarter of the total fall below trend. Much the greater part of the fall was therefore due to other factors than oil and gas.

The National Institue of Economic and Social Research in 1979 estimated the value of oil and gas output in 1980 at £12.2 thousand millions (National Institute Economic Review, Nov. 1979, p. 58). Of this, however, £3.5 thousand millions was to be directly remitted abroad as a return on foreign investments. Of the remainder, £5.2 thousand millions was to accrue to the U.K. Government by way of various taxes or 'abnormal' prfits, and this may be regarded as an approximate estimate of the 'pure gain' (but see further below in regard to terms of trade effects). The rest, £3.5 thousand millions, presumably consisted of direct payments to U.K. factors of production to produce the oil and gas[1].

Let us for simplicity assume that, apart from oil and gas, there are only two kinds of production in the U.K. : traded and non-traded goods and services. Let us further previsionally equate traded goods and services with manufacturing (this

---

[1] This is how it is treated in the following analysis. However, some of this sum may consist of a 'pure gain' accruing to consumers of gas, since the output of gas has been valued here at the oil it replaced rather than at the (lower) selling price. In so far as it should have been treated as a 'pure gain', the result has been to overstate the fall in manufacturing output.

almost certainly understates the traded goods and services sector, since agricultural goods and many services are traded, and we return to this point below). Then we can estimate a maximum fall in manufacturing output due to oil and gas as follows.

First, consider the 3.5 thousand million payment to U.K. factors of production. If there were no change in relative prices, and if resources were perfectly mobile, the diversion of these resources into production of traded goods (i.e. oil and gas) would simply reduce other output of traded goods (i.e. manufacturing) by an equal amount, assuming that factor costs would tend to lower their prices in relation to non-traded goods (the exchange rate would appreciate), and so demand would switch to some extent in favour of traded goods. The fall in manufacturing production would then be less than £3.5 thousand million.

Next, consider the £5.2 thousand million 'pure gain', and assume that the Government remits taxes, or else lends out the money, so that private consumption or investment rise by this amount altogether (with the present Government it seems reasonable to assume no increase in public expenditure). The rise in these expenditures will tend to increase imports and also increase the demand for manufacturing output. Using the latest (1972) input-output table available, and assuming that average and marginal propensities are equal, one can estimate that about 45 per cent of the extra demand would be for tradeables. The rest, about £2.9 million, would be for non-tradeables and, assuming no change in relative prices and mobile resources, would result in a fall of manufacturing output and a rise of non-tradeable output of this amount. Again, allowing for relative price changes should reduce the required fall in manufacturing output.

Taking both effects together, the maximum fall in manufacturing output is 3.5 + 2.9 = £6.4 thousand million, which is about 10 per cent of the value of manufacturing output in 1980 had it been 'on trend'. This 'trend' value is simply the projection of the average rate of growth in output from 1966-67 to 1973-74 on to 1980. Actual output in 1980 was 27 per cent below this trend value. Hence the maximum effect of oil and gas accounts for 10/27 = 37 per cent of the drop in manufacturing output below trend.

This, however, considerably exaggerates the likely effect. In the first place, in 1972 only about a half of exports of goods and services, after deducting their import content,

In the first place, in 1972 only about a half of exports of goods and services, after deducting their import content, consisted (directly or indirectly) of manufacturing output. If we then relate the £6.4 thousand millions above to a trend 'tradeables' output of £128 thousand millions in 1980, instead of one of £64 thousand millions confined to manufacturing, the maximum proportionate drop in tradeables output due to oil and gas is halved from 10 to 5 per cent. This may exaggerate the size of the tradeable sector. On the other hand the estimate is still too big since it neglects the fact that the figure of £6.4 thousand million should be reduced because, with tradeables now being defined more widely than manufacturing, the 'pure gain' would increase the demand for tradeables by more than was allowed for above. Furthermore, we must allow for the effect of some other factors. Thus, secondly, if relative prices are allowed to change the resulting switch in demand must favour tradeables output. Indeed, if resources were mobile and there were no relative price change there would be no problem – the contraction of manufacturing would then be quite painless. Thirdly, we should allow for the possibility that some of the 'pure gain' would be invested abroad. In so far as this occurs, no switch in domestic output is required – the immediate effect is similar to the remittances abroad which we have already deducted. The Government removed exchange controls on capital movements in 1979 at least partly because of the strong exchange rate, and so some offset here has certainly occurred. Finally, we should note that, in so far as there is a switch which requires some appreciation of the exchange rate, the terms of trade tend to improve. This adds to the 'pure gain' for the U.K. (sat other countries' expense), and to some extent increases the drop in tradeables output.

Taking account of all these factors, and especially the wider definition of tradeables, it seems unlikely that more than about a fifth of the drop in manufacturing output below trend in 1980 could be attributed to oil and gas, leaving over four fifths to be explained by other factors.

REFERENCES

C. Alsopp and V. Joshi, 1980, "Alternative Strategies for the U.K.", National Institute Economic Review, January.

F. Blackaby (ed), 1978, British Economic Policy 1960-74, Cambridge University Pres for the National Insitute of Economic and Social Research, Cambridge.

F. Blackaby (ed), 1980, The Future of Pay Bargaining, National Institute of Economic and Social Research, Joint Studies in Public Policy 2, Heinemann, London.

Cambridge Department of Applied Economics, 1975, 1976, 1977, 1978, 1979, 1980, Cambridge Economic Policy Review.

G. Davies, 1979, "The Effects of Government Policy on the Rise in Unemployment", London School of Economics and Political Science, Centre for Labour Economics, mimeo.

S.J. Nickell, 1979, "The Effect of Unemployment and Related Benefits on the Duration of Unemployment", Economic Journal, vol. 89.

E.H. Phelps Brown, 1975, "A Non-monetarist View of the Pay Explosion", Three Banks Review, No. 105.

M. FG. Scott with R.A. Laslett, 1978, Can We Get Back to Full Employment?, MacMillan, London.

M. FG. Scott, W.M. Corden and I.M.D. Little, 1980, The Case Against General Import Restrictions, Trade Policy Research Centre, Thames Essay, London.

C.T. Taylor and A.R. Threadgold, 1979, 'Real' national saving and its Sectoral Composition, Bank of England, Discussion Paper No. 6.

J.B. Wood, 1972, How Much Unemployment?, Institute of Economic Affairs, Research Monograph No. 28.

COMMENTS ON SCOTT'S PAPER
Richard Jackman, London School of Economics

Maurice Scott's paper provides a valuable and wide-ranging account of the unemployment debate in the U.K. While I agree with most of what he has to say, I think his main conclusion, that the higher levels of unemployment recently experienced can be associated with increased labour militancy, is not adequately supported by the evidence. While the immediate cause of higher unemployment is depressed demand, more fundamental, as Scott's paper clearly shows, is the shift in the inflation/unemployment trade-off. Even with unemployment in the 1970s far in excess of the post-war average, increases in aggregate demand have led to accelerating inflation. The question is why a shift in the trade-off should have occurred. It may be helpful to examine the various possible hypotheses within a common analytical framework.

A Suggested Framework'

The inflation/unemployment trade-off can be represented as in equation (1):

$$\dot{w} = \dot{p}^e + f(u - u_e) + z, \quad f' < 0 \qquad \ldots \ldots \quad (1)$$

where w is the rate of increase of money wages, p expected price inflation, u the actual and u_e the equilibrium of unemployment, and z represents "non-market" wage-push factors. The equilibrium rate of unemployment, u , consists of frictional and voluntary unemployment consistent with an overall balance of supply and demand in the labour market.

The unemployment rate consistent with non-accelerating inflation (known as NAIRU) is the value of u, denoted u_n , at which $\dot{w} = \dot{p}$ in equation (1).
Therefore

$$u = u_n - f^{-1}(z) \qquad \ldots \ldots \quad (2)$$

An increase either in equilibrium unemployment or (because f' < 0) in wage push increases the unemployment rate consistent with non-accelerating inflation.

We can, however, attempt to discriminate between different possible explanations if we write equation (1) in terms not of unemployment rates but of vacancy rates:

$$\dot{w} = \dot{p}_e + g(v - v_e) + z \qquad g' > 0 \qquad \ldots \ldots \quad (1')$$

FIGURE I.

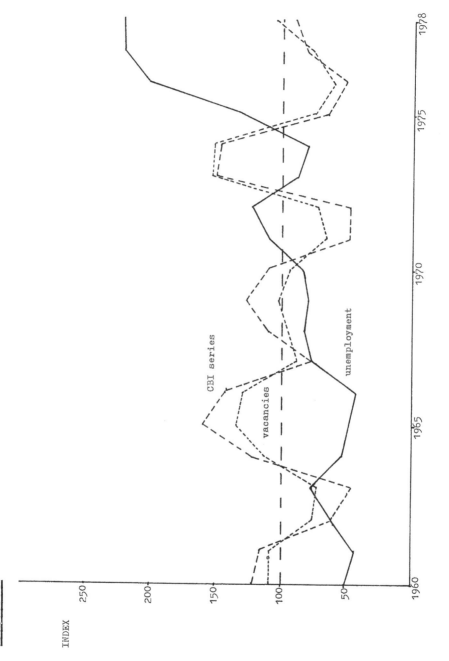

INDEX

250

200

150

100

50

1960   1965   1970   1975   1978

CBI series

vacancies

unemployment

where v is the actual and v the equilibrium rate of vacancies,
the latter being the "frictional" vacancies which are the
counterpart of frictional unemployment when the labour market
is in overall balance. The vacancy rate consistent with non-
accelerating inflation, v , is given by

$$v_n = v_e - g^{-1} (z) \qquad \qquad \ldots \ldots (2')$$

which increases if the equilibrium rate of vacancies goes up,
but decreases with an increase in wage push. We can now list
the various possibilities in Table 1.

TABLE 1
Effects on unemployment and vacancies

	Effect on	
	u	v
Increase in frictional unemployment	up	up
Increase in voluntary unemployment	up	unchanged
Increased "wage push"	up	down

The actual course of unemployment and vacancies over the
last 20 years is shown in Figure 1. Both unemployment and
vacancies are measured as an index with their average value
over the period set equal to 100. Two independent series for
vacancies are shown in Figure 1, vacancies registered at
employment offices and the "CBI variable", the proportion of
manufacturing firms reporting that their output was restricted
by a shortage of skilled labour. Neither series is an entirely
satisfactory measure of total vacancies in the labour market,
but the fact that both, though independently compiled, show a
similar picture suggest it may be a reasonably accurate one.
Clearly, there is a high degree of cyclical correspondence
between the three series in Figure 1, but whereas the two
vacancy series show little, if any, trend over the period,
there is marked upward trend in unemployment. Inflation, as
shown in Table 1 of Scott's paper, has accelerated over the
period, and especially in the early 1970s. The relationship
between changes in the inflation rate and the level of
vacancies presents a rather confusing picture, mainly because
the measures of price and wage inflation are strongly
influenced in the short run by incomes policies, exchange rate
changes and the like. One might want to argue that there is

now a greater tendency for inflation to increase at a given level of vacancies than has been the case in the past. But the evidence is not at all clear. For example, in terms of vacancies the recession of 1975-77 was similar to that of 1971-73, but the fall in inflation much greater in the more recent recession. In the absence of more convincing evidence, I will assume that there has been no change over the period in the relationship between vacancies and inflation, from which it follows that v can be assumed not to have changed over the period. From this it follows that by 1978, labour markets were, approximately, in equilibrium, and the high levels of unemployment cannot be explained in terms of a low pressure of demand, as implied by the wage push hypothesis.

It may be helpful therefore to reconsider some of the other hypotheses discussed in Scott's paper.

Frictional Unemployment

More frictional unemployment would imply more frictional vacancies, and given that vacancies have remained at quite a high level up to 1978, an increase in labour market mis-matching appears to be a plausible explanation.

Frictional unemployment is often linked to the idea of structural change in the economy, so the first is to find some way of measuring whether the amount of such structural change in the economy has in fact been increasing. One can argue that the increase in the world oil price in 1973 (and again in 1979) led to relative price "shocks" of an exceptional magnitude, which might in turn have required abnormally large structural changes (from energy using to energy saving industries) to accommodate them.

However, the evidence does not appear to support this argument. Nickell has calculated indices of regional and occupational job matching, which measure the imbalance between vacancy and unemployment rates by region and by occupation (S. Nickell, "The determinants of equilibrium unemployment in Britain" Centre for Labour Economics Discussion Paper No. 78). The regional index suggests that, if anything, regional unemployment and vacancy rates have been more closely matched since 1973 than previously. The occupational index, for data reasons, only starts in 1973, but it too shows no subsequent deterioration.

Related evidence (also presented by Nickell) is that the rate of decline in the proportion of the labour force employed in the production industries in the five years after 1973 was no more rapid than the rate of decline during the previous five years. While, of course, none of these measures is ideal, taken together they must cast considerable doubt on the view that labour market mis-matching has increased.

Since 1978 (the end of Nickell's data period), the U.K. economy has been affected to an increasing extent by the impact of North Sea Oil. North Sea Oil, which has an effect rather like scattering foreign currency from one of Professor Friedman's helicopters, forces up the exchange rate and thus leads to a shift in the industrial structure from traded to non-traded goods. Such a shift might generate higher than usual frictional unemployment, but it obviously cannot explain the increase in unemployment up to 1978. (On the other hand, North Sea Oil probably is a major factor in explaining why the present U.K. government's deflationary measures have had such a disproportionately severe impact on the manufacturing sector.)

Wage-push Factors

It would be difficult to deny that organised labour has become more powerful and more militant in recent years, but it does not follow that such increased militancy is best represented by an upward shift in money wage equations such as (1) or (1'). Let us first consider a model in which prices are a constant mark-up on wages, so that

$$\dot{p} = \dot{w} \tag{3}$$

substituting (3) into (1) gives

$$\dot{p} - \dot{p}^e = f(u - u_e) + z \tag{4}$$

Then an increase in z raised money wages in each sector, leading to price increases in each sector with the outcome an (unanticipated) increase in inflation. With adaptive expectations, inflation will accelerate, until the government introduces deflationary policies which increase unemployment. Real wages have not increased in this process and all the unions have achieved by the process is higher inflation and higher unemployment. Though the pursuit of higher money wages may be individually rational for each group of workers, it is collectively self-defeating.

A difficulty with the above description of the inflationary process is that it assumes that unions do not correctly anticipate the consequences of each other's actions and are always surprised by the increase in inflation that results. If, instead, we were to assume that workers form expectations rationally, and forecast each other's actions correctly, then, on average, p^e and p would be the same, and there would be no expected benefits from wage push.

A different approach is to assume that workers use their increased power to improve their real wages not at the expense of other sectors (which will not work) but at the expense of profits in their own sector. That is, the unions may instead be attempting to reduce the mark-up of prices over wages. If the mark-up (m) is allowed to vary, we can rewrite equations (3) and (4) as

$$\dot{p} = \dot{w} + \dot{m} \tag{3'}$$

$$(\dot{p} - \dot{p}^e) - m = f(u - u_e) + z \tag{4'}$$

To the extent that workers direct their efforts to reducing the mark-up, their concern is with "real" variables and hence will not impinge on the inflation/unemployment trade-off.

This leads to the argument which is often heard that unemployment is high because real wages are too high. Real wages may be too high either because of union militancy or because of a failure of the labour market to adjust sufficiently to the OPEC oil price increase, which might well require a fall in "equilibrium" real wages. One description of the relationship between real wages and unemployment is based on the idea that product prices are set in competitive markets and that firms operate on their (downward sloping) demand for labour curves. Such a model suggests that an increase in output requires a fall in the real wage. Given the assumption that wage bargaining will not permit a fall in the real wage, an increase in demand can only lead to inflation. While there is, presumably, in some long-run sense, a relationship between real wages and employment of this type, it is not very plausible in a cyclical context. An increase in demand in the short-run is more likely to be associated with a rise than with a decline in real wages, so that it is hard to see how real wage rigidities can prevent an expansion of output in the short-run.

A second model is based on the idea that high real wages may reduce international competitiveness. A high level of money wages in the U.K. relative to world prices may raise the price of U.K. goods (again relative to world prices) leading to reduced market shares for U.K. goods and hence less employment. (Because the real wage in this model is defined in terms of world prices, a depreciation of the exchange rate cannot improve competitiveness.) The main problems with this model are that it seems able only to explain the distribution of unemployment between countries, rather than simultaneous increases in all countries, and, secondly, that it predicts that a shock affecting all countries in common, such as the oil price increase, would have no impact on unemployment. A further problem with this theory as far as the U.K. is concerned is that its international competitiveness actually improved in the ten years up to 1977.

It is worth noting that this second model has much in common with the Cambridge Economic Policy Group model discussed in Part 3 of Scott's paper. Whether or not the government is worried about the trade balance, any expansion of demand will lead to a depreciation of the exchange rate, higher wage claims and hence accelerating inflation. The Cambridge Group seem to think that import controls are the answer in these circumstances, but their reasoning is hard to follow as Scott shows. In any event the model, with its emphasis on international competitiveness, cannot account for a simultaneous increase in unemployment in all countries.

A third possible mechanism operates through investment. Scott, in section 4 of his paper, distinguished "labour-using" and "labour-saving" investment. However, the same sort of mechanism can be examined within a standard putty-clay model. A high real wage both leads to a more capital intensive technology being embodied in new investment, and leads to a more rapid scrapping of old machines as they become unprofitable. Thus insufficient new jobs are created for the workers laid off from the machinery that has been scrapped. The immediate difficulty with this line of argument, as Scott acknowledges, is that it implies an increase in the growth of labour productivity, contrary to what has been observed.

Thus it appears that there are serious objections to each of the "labour militancy" or "excessive real wage" explanations, and all suffer from the problem sketched out in section I, namely that they imply that higher unemployment should be accompanied by fewer job vacancies.

Voluntary Unemployment

By voluntary unemployment we mean changes in the duration of unemployment or in the propensity to register for unemployment benefit induced by changes in the level of benefits or similar factors.

Unemployment in the U.K. is measured as the number of people registering as unemployed, which they need to do if they are to collect their unemployment benefits. People not entitled to benefits will not normally register, and thus will not count as unemployed in the statistics.

Until recently, married women were allowed to "opt out" of the national insurance system, and those who did opt out were not eligible for unemployment benefits. Hence, if they were unemployed they would not have registered, and therefore would not have been included in the statistics. An increasing proportion of married women are now in the national insurance scheme and hence have an incentive to register if unemployed.

Since 1960, the number of women registered as unemployed has risen more than twice as rapidly as the number of men, presumably largely because more unemployed women are now eligible for benefits. Given that the registered female unemployment may bear little relation to the "true" rate, it seems more sensible to focus on male unemployment, where these complications do not arise. Even so, the male unemployment rate has approximately trebled between the early 1960s and the late 1970s.

We next consider the effects of unemployment benefits. Scott argues that benefits cannot have been an important factor in part basing his argument on Nickell's estimates (Economic Journal, 1979). Nickell showed that the duration of unemployment spells was in fact quite sensitive to the "replacement rate" (the ratio of unemployment benefit to net of tax earnings), with an estimated elasticity of 0.6 to 1. The reason he argued that unemployment benefits could not explain much of the increase in unemployment was that the replacement ratios themselves had not increased at all significantly over the period.

However, the replacement rate can be measured in a number of different ways. The argument that it has not increased is normally based on measuring it as the ratio of an unemployed man's benefit entitlement to his net earnings in work. Nickell's estimates, however, are based on a family income measure, comparing total family income with the husband in work or unemployed. With married women's earnings an increasing proportion of family income, the replacement ratio, as defined in Nickell's paper, tends to rise even with no change in benefit rates. For example, there might be a little less pressure on school-leavers to take jobs where there are already two incomes in the family. Indeed, higher incomes (and benefit levels) may be a cause of higher unemployment through their income effect (rather than the replacement rate substitution effect usually considered).

A further factor has been stressed by Richard Layard. Before 1973 it was more common for people claiming social security to have their claim turned down on the grounds that they had refused to take jobs. People refused benefits have, of course, a much stronger incentive to find a job, and even if they are unsuccessful they have no incentive to continue to register as unemployed. A policy of refusing benefits thus reduces the measured (and probably the actual) rate of unemployment. Since 1973 the proportion of new unemployment claimants (deflated by available vacancies) denied benefit has fallen to about one-quarter of the pre 1973 level, and this softer line will have increased the measured (and probably the actual) rate of unemployment.

While it is hard to be entirely persuaded that these factors, even taken together, can explain the whole of the increase in the unemployment rate (up to 1978) it does seem that the equilibrium rate of unemployment may be significantly higher than the 2.7 per cent maximum suggested in Scott's paper.

Conclusions

The present government has brought about a sharp further rise in unemployment by following severely deflationary monetary policies. The hope that this might induce "realism" in wage bargaining has been confounded by the fact that wage increases have accelerated to an average rate of over 20%. A major reason seems to have been that the government has not appreciated the implications of its monetary policy for public sector pay, and the wage round has been characterised by a number of the grossly excessive public sector wage increases which the private sector has felt obliged to follow. In a slightly different terminology, private inflation expectations seem to have been influenced more by public sector pay increases than by the money supply targets, and, perhaps, rationally so.

While I have argued that demand deficiency has not been a major factor behind the growth in U.K. unemployment in the past, there is, unfortunately, little doubt that it is the main issue now and for the next few years. If, as Scott says, the new policies confront everyone with the real issue in wage bargaining, it is regrettable that the government appears to be the last to realise what those issues are. As a result, inflation is likely to continue, demand to remain depressed, and unemployment to continue to rise.

THE UNEMPLOYMENT POLICY DISCUSSION IN GERMANY IN THE 1970s

Harald Gerfin, University of Konstanz, Germany

In 1980 the German unemployment rate was around 3.5 percent. Such a figure does not look extraordinarily high in a longer-term perspective and even less so in present-day international comparisons. However, it is a startling level as compared to what happened in the period preceding the oil shock in 1973/74. During the 1960s and early 1970s – for nearly one and a half decades – Germany experienced unemployment rates only slightly fluctuating around an average of .7/.8 percent with the single exception of 1967/68. The first real post-war recession turned out to be short and mild : the annual unemployment rate reached a maximum of 1.7 percent in 1967, and the former level – officially proclaimed as the policy goal at that time – was already re-established by 1969.

Viewed against this background, the worsening of the labour market situation after 1973 appears rather dramatic in magnitude as well as in duration. Unemployment quintupled to a rate of more than 4 percent in 1975 and has not fallen much since then. As a consequence, "unemployment has been a major policy issue" in Germany as "in all (other) Western countries for over five years" (quotations from the preface to the programme of this seminar), and it has, indeed, "stirred significant theoretical controversy" (ibid.) in my country as it did elsewhere.

Many observers shared the opinion that unemployment of the size reached in 1975, if prolonged over a considerable time span, could or even would necessarily lead to social consequences which would jeopardize the survival of our economic (and political) system. This fear has proved groundless. Despite all hardships, social stability has never been endangered. On the contrary, a process of habituation to the high level of unemployment is evident, though opposed by many (including myself). It is an illuminating fact that the unemployment phenomenon was treated as a third order problem in our federal election campaign, the concern not being due to the prevailing level but to expected further deterioration in the near and the more distant future.

For an understanding of the actions of the public authorities and the reactions of the population, organized groups, etc., it is essential to remember the well known fact that Germans are traditionally more sensitive to inflation than the people of most other Western countries. If confronted with a stable modified Phillips curve, a "menu of choice" à la Samuelson/Solow, a majority would probably vote for a point close to zero inflation - to be bought by an unemployment rate well above the realized figures before and after the 1967/68 recession. Moreover, it seems that a widespread distrust of a stable Phillips relation existed in Germany long before the publication of Friedman's and Phelps' influential articles : people sub-consciously believed in the "natural rate of unemployment" proposition including its policy prescription of fighting inflation by creating more than "natural" unemployment for some time.

Both the 1967/68 and the 1974/75 recessions had been preceded by accelerating inflation. The authorities - the Federal Government as well as the (independent) central bank - tried to check this process by putting on the brakes sharply, deliberately accepting rather substantial effects on the demand for labour. Without exaggeration it can be said that both recessions were consciously accepted in order to get back to price stability. It is at least equally obsious that the restrictive measures were highly welcomed by the large majority of people, institutions and organized groups even after the labour market consequences had become visible. As the Sachverständigenrat, our Council of Economic Advisers, wrote in its 1967 annual report (p. 126), "it appeared as a cleaning thunderstorm if not as the long desired expiation of former intemperance... The call for sacrifice got more popular than ever before in the history of the Federal Republic". It is worth noting that, in the mid-sixties, an inflation rate slightly above three percent was considered alarming. The treatment proved succesful. Inflation had already slowed down from 3.6 percent in 1966 to 1.6 percent in 1967, remaining at that level for the rest of the decade.

Quite in accordance with the predominant attitudes sketched above, the prompt success on the price front did not lead to significant efforts to reduce the social costs of the cure in terms of unemployment, foregone national product, and possible induced impediments to economic development in the longer run. Based on rather broad agreement within society, the authorities were hesitant to change their policy measures in an expansionary direction. Claims for such a change conflicted, as the Sachverständigenrat pointed out (in its 1967 report already mentioned, p. 122), with the "deeply rooted aversion against any kind of overall demand stimulating policies by the government". Even within the business sector the situation was mostly not interpreted as a recession characterized by a general lack of demand but as a cumulation of sectoral crises calling for selective assistance instead of global activating measures which had been advoceated at that time, among some others, by the Sachverständigenrat. Besides the structural argument there was, on the whole, a strong confidence in the effectiveness of free market forces to restore growth and to bring back employment to an optimal level without intolerable delay, provided only that the self-regulating process was not blocked by a policy of the unions leading to excessive wage increases.

Nevertheless, in the course of 1967 the Federal Government (with Karl Schiller as Minister of Economics) enacted, successively, two public expenditure programs. Though small in dimension relative to the size of idle capacity, they certainly contributed to the process of recovery without, however, helping very much to remove the widespread aversion against such measures in principle. They looked superfluous, if not dangerous, in the light of the following development : a strong, unexpected increase of foreign demand starting in 1968 and a subsequent explosive growth of private investment – a cyclical pattern as in former upswings – led to one of the heaviest postwar booms restoring full employment in 1969 and eliminated the seemingly structural (sectorial, regional, etc.) problems. The boom was also highly favourable to profits. During the recession, workers and unions had been very modest in their wage claims, a behaviour facilitated by the official promise to ensure "social symmetry" after regaining prosperity. So workers and unions felt deeply duped and fought for a fairer income share. The resulting distributional conflict was the sharpest in postwar history. Since it occurred under conditions of general excess demand at home as well as rapidly increasing prices all over the Western world, it reestablished major inflationary pressures. These developments during the late 1960s turned out to be a big burden in the following years.

As already pointed out, the recession following 1973 was also policy-induced. Of course, it was not intended to produce such a deep and lasting crisis as materialized, but major restrictive measures seemed indispensable to practically everybody. Inflation had accelerated continuously despite a temporary slowdown of activity in 1971/72. In 1973, consumer prices rose by 7 percent, twice as fast as in 1966. Even higher rates were generally expected and their anticipation in wage and other contracts nearly guaranteed their occurence as long as things were allowed to slide. Advanced as the evil was, its elimination required drastic treatment with painful consequences.

The Bundesbank started the battle in Winter 1972/73 by rigorously reducing the money supply (flanked by measures to avoid capital imports) thereby pushing the interest rate to a two-digit level and forcing banks into quantitative credit rationing. The Federal Government followed soon thereafter. In Spring 1973, it imposed an additional tax on both (higher) private and corporate incomes (10 percent), a tax on investment (11 percent) and a severe reduction of depreciation allowances. Furthermore, it was decided to reduce public investment expenditures.

This bundle of monetary and fiscal restraints was expected to stop the price spiral and the persistence of a generally restrictive course to cut inflation to a tolerable level within a couple of years. The induced unemployment, though probably of significant magnitude, was taken to be transitory and, given the coverage and level of social security, considered socially bearable. Longer-term projections by public authorities, business, unions, independent research institutes etc., all agreed at that time in concluding that the forces of economic growth would remain powerful during the 1970s, implying a lasting trend towards a strong demand for labour in excess of domestic supply, even taking account of the sizable expected increase in domestic labour supply after fifteen years of decline. Hence, a temporary slackening of labour demand did not look too threatening. Moreover, the high and fast growing stock of foreign workers imported hitherto to fill the domestic labour supply gap had raised a feeling of discomfort and there were major objections to a prolongation of that policy. Consequently, recruitment of workers from abroad was stopped in the fall of 1973 - immediately after the labour market first showed signs of relaxation. This ban has been contined. It reduced, over the years, the number of foreign workers by more than half a million people.

The question of whether or not the demand restraints would have proved successful under normal circumstances, interesting as it would be in principle, can be left open. The special design of the programme - its concentration on discouragement of private investment – gives rise to some doubts. But whatever the outcome might have been, the explosion of oil prices in 1973/74 changed matters significantly. To be sure, this external supply shock alone could have been absorbed without a major set-back if all groups had been prepared to accept their shares in the decline of overall domestically disposable income. As it turned out, this was not the case. The unions – as in the bargaining round of 1973 when they still trusted in the former "full employment guarantee" and, therefore, did not realize the degree of commitment of the authorities to beat down inflation – in 1974 again pushed up standard wages by a two-digit rate in order to withhold the impact of the OPEC measures from the workers and to improve their real wage position even further. The employers, on the other hand, did not resist the claims very strongly. Obviously, they believed they could pass on the higher costs to prices. However, they had overestimated this possibility.

The authorities stuck to their decision to give priority to reestablishement of price stability and, therefore, tried to eliminate the scope for passing on costs. While the central bank continued its tight money policy, the fiscal authorities did abolish the additional tax burdens but, at the same time, they depressed public expenditures even further.

As a result, the exogenous (and internally intensified) cost push was prevented from speeding up inflation in contrast to what had been widely feared. The rate of price increase was stopped in 1974 and lowered successively thereafter, in total by not less than 4 1/2 percentage points until 1978 before it turned for the worse again.

Real GNP, on the other hand, having grown to an average rate of 4 1/2 percent in the early seventies (as in the decade before) and 5 percent in 1973, came to a nearly complete halt in 1974 and declined by roughly 2 percent in 1975 – a phenomenon never observed before in post-war years. Employment diminished by 5 1/2 percent within these two years despite some temporary labour hoarding by firms (the subsequent elimination of which led to severe misinterpretations : the fact that emplyment reductions went on well after output had turned up made many observers believe that the normal relationship between growth and employment did not hold any more – the so-called "uncoupling hypothesis", an erroneous and politically misguided view).

The rapid increase of unemployment and the growing doubts of employees as to the security of their jobs induced households to expand their savings rate so that even private consumption failed to support aggragate product demand considerably.

All these developments were extremely unfavourable to private investment. Having been weak (or, more precisely, weakened by political measures) already in 1973, its share in GNP dropped by another 3 percentage points in real terms (4 points in nominal terms) until 1975 - a process which, of course, contributed markedly to the slack in overall demand. Investors faced a severe profit squeeze as well as an unprecedented degree of unused productive capacity (the utilization rate was down to only slightly over 90 percent in 1975 compared to a former average of more than 97 percent, according to the estimates of the Sachverständigenrat).

Registered unemployment reached 4.1 percent, but it was well exceeded by the underutilization rate of potential labour input - 5.4 percent in terms of manyears and 9 percent in terms of manhours, the latter corresponding with the degree of idle productive capacity. The situation was really horrifying, keeping in mind the still very fast inflation.

I admit, of course, that public policy was confronted with a fundamental dilemma. Anti-inflation policy cannot succeed without demand restraint at least as one of its central elements. If inflationary pressures develop a self-perpetuating momentum there is probably no other option than to keep the brakes on until all groups have been harmed sufficiently and evidently as to eliminate the belief that one's own hardships are due to the inflationary excesses of others which require defensive or even aggressive counter-action. Such shock treatment is, of course, much more complicate and socially expensive if the sources of the disturbance are not under domestic control but external as in the case of the oil price increase. Since, on the one hand, the need to get rid of inflation was more or less beyond dispute or dissent in Germany and, on the other hand, there was a basic understanding that the return to price stability must involve costs, the recession of 1974/75 did not itself cause major controversies or conflicts. Of course, when unemployment approached and then passed the one million mark, there were headlines in the newspapers, discussions in TV programmes, etc. but, on the whole, it was accepted as a cathartic process -even more widely so than in the much less pronounced recession of the mid-sixties when voting behaviour changed dramatically in favour of the extreme right-wing National Democratic Party.

Severe theoretical and political controversies burst out only when the new cyclical upswing which started at the end of 1975 had gone on for a while without reducing but merely stabilizing the high level of unemployment. The longer the poor labour market conditions lasted, the more and heavier quarrels arose about the obstacles to a return to full employment as well as the adequacy of recipes for overcoming the problem. There was (and still is) no theoretical or political view taken elsewhere in the Western world which did not find its advocates in Germany - with the single qualification of the general agreement on keeping down inflation. In the following, I will briefly report and comment on the main positions held in the discussion.

In 1978, Kurt Rothschild published a paper titled "Unemployed : Are There Any?" (1). This intentionally exasperating title spotlights obviously increasing endeavours by orthodox academic economists, some politicans, employers and their organisations, etc., to contest the existence of major employment problems. There are, on the other hand, groups with the opposite proclivity to overstate matters, but their influence on published and public opinion has been comparatively weak.

It cannot be denied, of course, that the official unemployment statistics of all countries - regardless whether they are based on registrations with the labour offices (as in Germany) or on household surveys - are subject to distortions in both directions and, therefore, given room for alternative interpretations according to specific interests.
In the recent past, the "shirkers and freeriders" - hypothesis has received a rather prominent role in the dispute. It asserts that a large fraction of the persons registered as unemployed is in fact not looking for jobs but just exploiting benefits offered by the social security system. Doubtless such cases do exist. Any security system runs the risk of being misused, and it is obvious that the chances of misuse are larger in slack rather than tight labour markets. The size of this "unreal" component, however, is rather small in Germany as empirical investigations show. The Institute for Employment Research calculated for 1977 the number of registered unemployed with personal characteristics enabling them to profit from the security system though unwilling to work at not more than 84 000 persons, representing 8 percent of total registered unemployed, but it is highly implausible to assume

On the other hand, a large number of potential workers do not enter the unemployment statistics. They do not register with the labour offices because they are temporarily discouraged, but they belong to the labour force since they are ready to return to employment as soon as jobs become available. In Germany, not a few observers are inclined to ignore this hidden unemployment andd stress the hypothetical character of quantification procedures. But despite indisputable measurement problems, it is evident from historical experience that slack labour markets produce a substantial Stille Reserve, as we call it. According to the most convincing estimates, this reserve jumped to almost half a million people in 1975 and increased to nearly 600 000 in 1977 before it began to decline somewhat to 430 000 in 1979. This is a multiple of that part of registered unemployment which can be classified as "unreal". The net bias of the official statistics is, therefore, definitely and significantly downward.

Rothschild's article referred to above is addressed mainly to another tranquilization strategy : the declaration of unemployment as mostly voluntary. The old-fashioned view that lasting unemployment must be voluntary, supposed to be dead for a long time, has found a seemingly fresh foundation in job search theories. The "new microeconomic theory" has its merits, but it can never be developed into a general theory of unemployment as is claimed by many of its advocates. It is misleading in situations of severe overall job shortage. A quintupled unemployment rate as in Germany during the second half of the seventies cannot be explained by voluntarily extended search activities. The majority of the unemployed would certainly accept jobs at the going wage rates immediately if they got an offer. In fact, most vacancies are filled very quickly. Even if a much higher number of people than before had deliberately prolonged search activities, the labour market problem as a whole or its political relevance would not be diminished since, by their behaviour, the chances of the others finding a job would be increased. It is, as Rothschild argues, relevant only as to who is first in getting one of the scarce jobs. The dimension of the problem is still appropriately measured by the sum of registered and hidden unemployment, corrected only for the "unreal" component dealt with in the last paragraph.

Having sketched some rather silly, though influential, arguments in the German discussion, let us turn to controversies which have to be taken seriously.

The first question is whether the labour market disturbances are basically structural in character or, at least predominantly attributable to a general insufficiency of labour demand.

"Structure" is a very ambiguous term. In some sense or another, every crisis may be labelled "structural". So discussions can be — and often are —terribly confused because the participants have different aspects in mind. But even if the suspected structural problem is specified, it remains difficult to test its relevance ex ante. Structural changes go on permanently though not steadily. The crucial point is, of course, whether the structural problems which appear in slack labour market situations would vanish in the course of a normal recovery of aggregate demand and, therefore, can be overcome by global stimulating measures, or whether they would hamper a return to full employment unless removed by selective intervention.

The original structuralist proposition emphasizes descrepancies in the special characteristics of labour demand and labour supply. This was the view of the opponents to demand promotion policies in the "great employment controversy" in the United States during the nearly sixties which was repeated in a similar fashion in Germany in the mid-seventies. It was asserted by many that the change in the sectoral structure of labour demand had accelerated rapidly bacause of fast shifts in product demand and/or disproportionate changes in technology leading to a severe mismatch of labour demand and supply by occupation, region etc. The Institute of Employment Research, however, demonstrated in 1976 that this presumption did not stand against empirical evidence. The speed of change of the sectoral structure — in terms of production as well as of employment — shows a significantly downward trend over the postwar period, superimposed by marked cyclical variations which, however, reversed their pattern around 1960. Before this benchmark year, high speed changes took place in prosperity periods whereas they occurred in recession phases afterwards. This fact, no doubt, increased the perception of structural problems in the more recent past since in boom periods they are resolved with much less friction. Comparing the last two recessions, changes in the sectoral structure were much more pronounced in 1967 than in 1974/75. In this respect, the acceleration thesis, therefore, is not confirmed — on the contrary. The same conclusion holds for the regional as well as the professional distribution of unemployment. These and other findings do not support the structuralist proposition though it must be admitted that they do not, as such, rule out the possibility of discrepancies between the qualitative characteristics of unemployed labour and the structure of additional demand forthcoming in the course of an upswing. But in the past even larger structural disturbances have proved to be no impediment to full employment.

Herbert Giersch and others from the Kiel Institute are exponents of quite another structural argument which has found wide acceptance. They stress the view that the German economy - protected by a lasting undervaluation of the German Mark - had for a long time failed to sufficiently reshape its productive structure leading to severe losses of growth and employment opportunities in the seventies after the appreciations of the Mark, the rise of the price of imported oil and of some raw materials, the increasing ability and pressure of developing countries to export manufactured goods to the developed ones etc. For them, the main problems result from overly slow instead of overly fast structural changes. This hypothesis sounds plausible. But it is hardly testable empirically and, even if true, does not imply that bottlenecks on the supply side of the labour market hamper the process of adjustment. The political conclusion is the call for growth promotion by means of generally improving the opportunities -and incentives for private investment and innovations leaving the direction of expansion to the enterprises and the market. Selective intervention is strictly rejected.

Deeper insights into the mechanisms and problems of the labour market were opened in the mid-seventies when (gross) flow statistics became available. They disproved - in many essential respects - widely held judgements based solely on stock figures. For the United States where labour turnover studies were carried out earlier, Robert Solow summarized their principal findings as follows : "What emerges from this sort of research is a rather unexpected picture of the labor market. It is as different as it can be from the old structuralist picture. The emphasis is not on a small (though perhaps growing) group of hard-core long-term unemployables who spend most of their time vainly looking for work. On the contrary, it appears that the group with the highest risk of unemployment - women, blacks, and young people - move back and forth between employment and unemployment rather frequently, and perhaps equally frequently into and out of the labor force.

In Germany, too, the general turnover rate is much more pronounced than had been commonly assumed before. Nearly 6 million people (a full quarter of the labour force) change firms every year, roughly half of them with unemployment episodes. In other words : about 3 million people enter the pool of unemployed each year, three times as many as the average stock figure, but, since the level of the pool lowered a bit after 1975, an even larger number got out of it, most of them (some 80 percent) into employment. Furthermore, quite a lot of the workers changing firms (with or without unemployment spells) move, at the same time, to other sectors of production and/or occupations as well as – to a less but significant amount – to other regions. The rapid turnover and its re-allocation characteristics (which cannot be spelled out in detail in this paper) point to a high degree of flexibility on both the supply and the demand side of the labour market.

Structural unemployment in the sense of an imbalance between job requirements and worker qualifications implies the simultaneous existence of long individual unemployment duration for workers with specific characteristics and of a considerable number of jobs with other characteristics remaining vacant over extensive periods. The overall picture in Germany looks quite different. In 1976 when the unemployment rate (in its national definition) amounted to 4,7 percent, nearly 15 percent of employees had spells of unemployment, many of them more than once, with an average duration of (completed) spells of 16 weeks. In the following years the duration did not lengthen. It was much longer than in the late 1960s and early 1970s (6–8 weeks), but this observation is not at all astonishing taking the vacancy figures into account. The average stock of vacancies-employment ratio which fluctuated around 3 percent before the recession dropped to 1.1 percent in 1975 and has kept this extremely low level since then. To a significant though minor degree, the reduction was due to fewer jobs becoming vacant (10 compared to 12–15 percent). Predominantly, it resulted from an acceleration in filling vacancies. They last, on average, only 5–6 weeks instead of 10–13 weeks in the preceding period.

These findings indicate that a persistent general job shortage is the outstanding problem. Nonetheless, there are, of course, particular demographic, geographic, and industrial segments of the labour market which suffer employment difficulties well above average. They differ widely, however, with regard to the frequency and the duration components. Some disadvantaged demographic groups including young as well as low-qualified people suffer from a high risk of becoming unemployed but, being hit, remain in the pool of unemployed for rather short time spans. Others, mainly older people, bear (by effective protection against lay-offs) a very limited risk of losing their jobs combined with an extremely high risk of long unemployment duration. A third group consisting of women (especially those looking for part time work), persons with restrictive health conditions, and workers with a cumulation of job chance-reducing characteristics is disadvantaged in both respects.

Similar divergencies have been discovered for geographic, industrial, and professional segments with regard to unemployment as well as vacancies. Each breakdown indicates cases of deficient labour demand, of deficient labour supply, of demand and supply mismatch and of unstable jobs or job-holding behaviour. However, the first category of unemployed – those suffering from a demand gap – stands out by far, both in terms of frequency as well as degree.

All these studies, though preliminary and in need of further elaboration, lead to the following general policy conclusions :

(1)   It is necessary to improve the allocative efficiency of the labour market mechanisms by extending the services of the labour administration system and making them more powerful. This is not to say that the major problems originate in defects of the search process, but there are still weaknesses causing foregone opportunities and, in particular, a highly unequal distribution of employment chances. This calls, over and above the need to strengthen information-providing activities, for selective pinpointed measures to overcome the specific problems of specially disadvantaged groups. In order to design them more appropriately than in the past, it is necessary to distinguish between cases of longer-term impediments on the one hand and of unstable employment on the other.

(2)   The instruments controlled by the labour administration authorities, important as they are, have but a very limited influence on labour demand and job creation. Therefore, general measures are required to close the large and, under status quo conditions, probably ever growing overall gap between labour demand and suppply. As historical experience in Germany and elsewhere shows and as is reconfirmed by a very recent regional cross-section analysis, overall improvements of labour market conditions help, by themselves, significantly to enlarge the re-

employment chances of disadvantaged groups (in Germany this holds especially for low qualified workers and, even more so, people with health problems).

Since in the course of longer-term excess labour supply structural hardening of unemployment typically increases, a return to full employment becomes more and more complicated the longer adequate measures are postponed.

Obviously, there are two basic options for eliminating a lasting excess labour supply : a stimulation of labour demand by growth promotion or a reduction of labour supply (or some combination of both). In the most recent past, a strong controversy arose as to which of these strategies should be given primary emphasis. The unions, a large fraction of the Social Democratic Party, a group of academic economists and some others stress the outstanding importance of cutting down – one way or another – the total average life-long work time in order to distribute short employment opportunities in a fair manner. Most advocates of this basic strategy are not in principle opposed to growth stimulation. Anti-growth attitudes have never been very influential in Germany, and the momentum of the movement diminished significantly during the period of slack labour markets – especially within the unions. Instead, there is – for different reasons – a deep scepticism of the possibility of reaching and maintaining a sufficient speed of growth as to absorb the already unemployed as well as the forthcoming additional supply (approximately one million people by the end of the decade). In my judgement, however, it is not realistic to expect a substantial contribution from the alternative, supply-reducing, strategy, simply because it does not seem feasable to accelerate the process of shortening work hours etc. considerably above its past, rather high trend rate – not at least in the next five years or so which is the relevant period since at the end of the 1980s the domestic labour force will start to decline again due to demographic reasons. Though an important issue in the current discussion, I confine myself to this scanty comment on it.

Between those favouring a strategy of employment expansion – by means of stimulating output, not by slowing down productivity growth – there are two other conflicting views, one of them stressing the level of the real wage rate as the limiting factor, the other one attributing unemployment to deficient product demeand. This controversy was by far the most excited quarrel in the employment debate during the last years. Only in the very recent past has it receded somewhat from the forefront of the battle.

To orthodox economists it is almost self-evident that a market can fail to clear only when the price in this particular market differs from its equilibrium level. This holds true, for them, for aggregate markets including the aggregate labour market. Such an interpretation sounds plausible a priori for the general public, and it looks even more convincing when a situation of unemployment was preceded by exceptional rates of wage increase like those of the early sevsesnties. So, a great many observers ascribed the persistence of high unemployment after 1975 to a level of real wages that made it unprofitable to expand output and employment in spite of large idle capacity. The single remedy, then, is a restrictive wage policy. This view was taken in the most provocative way by the Sachverständigenrat in its 1977/78 report which is crowded with statements like : "A more than transitory excess supply in the labour market must be caused by too high wages".

In the meantime it become better understood that the relationship between wages and employment depends on the demand-supply-constellation in the product market. Even the Sachverständigenrat concedes nowadays that the inverse relation holds only when the product market is either cleared or in excess demand and that - in a world of rather small and slow price reactions on demand or supply surpluses - the product market may well remain in excess supply over considerable periods of time. Under such a condition, the real wage rate may be at its labour market clearing level without re-establishing full employment. The amount of labour demand is determined by the insufficient strength of product demand (with multiplicative spillover effects between the two markets). One must distinguish, therefore, between the cases of "classical" unemployment (due to excessive real wages) and "Keynesian" unemployment (due to deficient product demand) - both being temporary (though possibly enduring) equilibria with quantity rationing. The self-curing mechanisms are probably much weaker in the Keynesian case in which both markets are in excess supply since prices are significantly more rigid in the downward than in the upward direction, leading to a stronger need for intervention by means of demand stimulating measures.

These considerations refer only to the theoretical possibilities. It is quite difficult to test empirically whether a concrete unemployment situation is (predominantly) of the classical or of the Keynesian type. The development of the last years, however, provides evidence for the Keynesian case. According to business surveys, in the period from 1976 - 78 only a very small minority of firms (some 5 percent) regarded wage costs as the reason for not fully using their technical capacities, whereas more than 40 percent attributed the lasting idleness to a lack of orders. The Sachverständigenrat confirmed the persistance of considerable deficient demand even of 1979 when the situation had improved somewhat. Wage cost pressures diminished continuously and significantly after 1974, reducing the real wage position to its pre-recession level rather quickly, accompanied by an appreciable drop of the rate of price inflation from 7 percent in 1973/74 to 2.6 percent in 1978. Nearly all observers agree that the wage policy of the social partners has fulfilled its task of avoiding "classical" obstacles to high employment in the recent past. Public policy, on the other hand, has failed to fulfil its task of removing "Keynesian" obstacles, and the authorities are not prepared to give up their waiting attitudes at present in spite of visible changes for the worse. They do not see, as they officially proclaim, a further need for action.

Besides the widespread aversion in principle against demand stimulating measures mentioned earlier, one argument for refraining from severe efforts in the current situation is the assertion that the instruments have proved ineffective. It is said that some dozen fiscal programs carried out since 1975 did not yield a notable decline of unemployment. I disagree with this argument. The unsatisfactory results are partly due to diversification into too many different, mostly small short-running measures which are unable to bring about perceptible changes of conditions and expectations. Furthermore, some of them were not directed to diminish the problem of overall excess labour supply. In such a situation, mobility incentives, assistence to some disadvantaged groups etc. cannot help, on the whole. On the other hand, some global budgetary measures – on the expenditure as well as on the tax side – have been taken too. Despite their relatively small scale, they definitely helped to promote the recovery of production in 1976 – which brought the unemployment increase to a halt – as well as the upswing of production and employment in 1978/79. However, the first signs of changes for the better caused the authorities to reverse their policy in order to reduce public deficits which led to a fresh feebleness of the economy in 1977 as well as in 1980. The reactions of production and employment to expansionary as well as contractive fiscal impulses demonstrate – in contrast to widespread belief – a strong influence of budgetary measures.

Nonetheless, official policy, the Sachverständigenrat and others are certainly right in stressing the necessity to reach a process of self-sustained growth based on private activity, especially on a steep and steady path of private, capacity-enlarging, innovation-bearing and job-creating investment. Measures which improve the supply side conditions for such a process must be welcomed all the more since they reduce inflationary tendencies. But the institutions mentioned tend to rely, in my judgement, too onesidely on providing better supply conditions. As long as idle capacities and slack demand persist they are probably of little avail. I therefore think that demand-stimulating measures are indispensable as well. All experience of the more recent post shows, furthermore, that the propensity to invest increases only after a considerable time span of expanding output and satisfactory rates of return. Small and short-run impulses are insufficient to build up stable, optimistic expectations and, thereby, to change the attitudes of investors. This leads to the prescription of announcing and conducting a longer-term stimulating strategy as long as product demand hampers the reattainment of high employment. Such a policy might be labelled a middle-range "conditional full employment guarantee" - conditional with regard to adequate wage contracts.

Several research institutes have developed programmes on these lines designed to remove unemployment by 1985. In practice, however, their chance of being realized is close to zero, at least in the near future. Even disregarding the fear of feeding inflation - which need not be the consequence - the large public debt accumulated over the years of slack activity (by built-in stabilizers as well as discretionary measures) is a politically powerful argument against any major expansive plan. The debt burden is felt to be much more threatening than unemployment at present. So-called "consolidation" of the public budgets (i.e. diminishing deficits) is ranked well above creation of labour demand. It is a narrow-minded view, however. A successful stimulating programme would lead - according to the calculations of the institutes - to a much lower increase in public debt than would materialize under status quo conditions, not to speak of the outcome of an even more restrictive course of fiscal policy. Nevertheless, probably no programme of that kind will be brought into action before unemployment reaches a level markedly higher than the present one.
The grand total conclusion must be a rather pessimistic view of the labour market prospects for the years to come.

Notes
(1) K. Rothschild, "Arbeitslose : Gibt's die?", Kyklos, 1, 1978.

COMMENTS ON GERFIN'S PAPER

Richard Layard, London School of Economics

I found this paper very interesting and also very
encouraging – it's always encouraging for the British to be
told that the Germans have problems. Unfortunately, I have an
excess supply of comments. So I will ration myself to two basic
issues about how labour markets work and then two briefer but
equally basic issues.

1. The Real Wage Issue

A major issue among economists has been whether
unemployment is what Malinvaud calls classical or what he calls
Keynesian. In both cases firms are thought of as competitive.
But in the classical case they are on their supply curves,
equating the marginal product of labour to the real wage,
whereas in the Keynesian case they are inside their supply
curves, being rationed by the insufficiency of the exogenous·
forces determining aggregate demand. The difference here is not
a narrow academic one but is of profound consequence for the
world. For if firms are on their supply curves then a concerted
reflation by all countries would inevitably lead to a world
inflation. So if you set up the model so that firms are always
on their supply curve, the real wage determines employment.
This is the model used for example in a sequence of papers by
Michael Bruno and Jeffrey Sachs, which are in many ways the
most serious attempt I have found of attempts to understand
what is happening to the OECD economy. But if firms are off
their supply curves and there is excess supply in product
markets, an international convoy is possible and desirable.

This is how the problem is generally posed. But I wonder
if either of the alternatives is plausible, in other words,
whether the perfect competition assumption is useful. As
regards Malinvaud's Keynesian unemployment which Professor
Gerfin believes in, I find the concept of excess supply in a
competitive goods market very difficult to imagine. What on
earth stops the price falling? I do not remember observing
differing tightness of the market for groceries or clothes over
the business cycle. It is only when prices are administered
that one experiences differing cyclical tightness – for example
for cars. But then administered pricing goes with imperfect
competition. And questions like "Is your output limited by lack
of orders?" only really make sense if there is imperfect
competition.

So one naturally asks : What in the presence of imperfect competition is the analogue to the distinction between classical and Keynesian unemployment? The answer, so far as I can see, is that there is no analogous distinction. Thinking of one firm, it has a marginal cost curve which depends on its money wage and a marginal revenue curve which depends on the incomes of its potential customers and the prices of its rivals. It equates marginal cost to marginal revenue at a quantity which will be higher the higher the incomes of its customers. In this model, the real product wage has no effect upon output — in fact the firm chooses the real wage when it chooses its price and output. If energy and capital and energy are sufficiently complementary, the share of wages could go up, when energy prices rise.

One could say this model too is unrealistic. One might say that workers choose the real wage. We can still handle this in an imperfect competition framework. Output and employment will then depend on the real wage, but also on customers' incomes.

I do not know how far one should be willing to abandon the competitive paradigm when doing macroeconomics, but it is clearly a matter with profound ideological implications. Perfect competition does not seem to make sense when one asks firms to say whether they have excess capacity due to lack of orders. And in parenthesis on the matter of questionnaire evidence any rational firm would always be as concerned about its wage costs as about its demand curve, so I am not impressed by Professor Gerfin's suggestion that money wages do not matter because in 1976-8, 40 per cent said they were constrained by lack of orders and only 5 per cent by wages. His argument takes one back to the old controversy between Machlup and Lester, where I think Machlup was right. Wages do obviously matter, but if firms are not on competitive supply curves, reflation is logically possible without an automatic increase in price inflation.

In any case, one of the puzzling features of the too high real wage story has always been that, if firms' supply of output is the constraint, the first reaction to an increase in nominal spending should be a rise in prices, with wages lagging, whereas in fact in Britain at any rate wages have generally lagged behind prices.

So my conclusion up to this point is that governments probably could physically increase output by reflation and the constraint is not that inflation will be generated in the goods market but that it may be generated in the labour market.

2. When to Deflate

This brings me to the second issue I want to discuss which relates to the process of wage formation. The question is : Suppose that prices in a country are raised by an external shock such as an oil price rise. Should the government accommodate its monetary policy or not? In 1974, Britain certainly did, but Germany did not. In 1979 both did.

It seems to me that the crucial issue in designing an optimal policy is the extent to which when negotiating wages, workers think about prices in a forward-looking or backward-looking way. If they are forward-looking the case against accommodation is very strong. For suppose there is an oil shock in year t. Then if workers are given the expectation of low inflation from t to t+1, they will in t settle for low wage increases, and these will be consistent with full employment in t+1 provided unemployment rises enough to depress their real wage claim sufficiently. If, however, there is a monetary accomodation then workers may be led to expect still higher money wages the following year and inflation will persist in the year after the oil shock.

Now consider the case where workers are backward-looking in the sense that price inflation affects their claim by making them seek compensation for past price increases. Then, once the inflation rate has gone up as the result of the oil shock, it cannot fail to be embodied in future inflation rates. Only umemployment will bring it down (assuming we have no incomes policy), and the optimal path of de-escalation is hardly likely to involve the degree of deflation practised in Germany in 1973/4.

Unfortunately, it is very difficult econometrically to distinguish between the forward-looking and backward-looking interpretations of wage formation, and in any case the answer may differ between countries. I can only say that in Britain at present the assumption that wages would be set in a forward-looking manner is not being born out very well.

3. The Workshy

I would now turn to two non-wage explanations of unemployment considered by Professor Gerfin. First there is the question of whether higher levels of unemployment benefit have increased unemployment. This is a question of changes not of levels. So I do not think figures of labour reserves are very relevant nor are figures of the proportion of unemployed people who are better off out of work than in work. Some people will work even if better off out of work, but many others will not work even if there is a net financial gain from work. We really need to know the elasticity of unemployment with respect to benefits. However, though it would be good to know the causes of unemployment, the crucial thing for macroeconomic policy is the relation between inflation and the tightness of the labour market. One clearly cannot assume tightness is measured by unemployment, but it could be measured by vacancies. I wuld therefore urge that in all labour market analysis much more attention be paid to the vacancy series, and I would love to be told how it has moved in Germany. In particular, has there been any period when the labour market was really tight since 1973? If there has been, I would doubt whether there has not been a substantial increase in voluntary unemployment. But my main worry is that the natural rate so clearly depends on the past levels of unemployment.

4. Structural Unemployment

Another explanation of increased unemployment is a more rapid rate of structural change. I was very happy to learn that the rate of change of the structure of production and employment has not increased in Germany; nor has it in Britain. That seems to me to clinch the question. But Professor Gerfin brings some other arguments that seem to me unsound. He argues that if there is a rapid turnover you cannot have structural unemployment. This does not seem to follow at all. For examle, suppose there are 100 building workers and 80 building jobs, one of which ends every day, making its occupant unemployed. The average duration of unemployment will only be 20 days, but the unemployment rate will be 20 per cent.

THE DUTCH EMPLOYMENT PROBLEM IN COMPARATIVE PERSPECTIVE

Angus Maddison, University of Groningen

The Dutch Labour Market Situation

The standard unemployment indicator in the Netherlands has been the rate derived by dividing the registered unemployed by the dependent population. This measure understates unemployment because certain people, willing to work and seeking jobs, are excluded. It is now possible, thanks to the E.E.C. labour force sample survey, to measure unemployment more comprehensively and relate it to the labour force (see Annex 1). Using the latter definition, unemployment averaged 1.9 per cent in the 1960-73 period and in 1974-9 rose to 5.9 per cent of the labour force. Thus unemployment increased sharply in the 1970s, and was higher than in other E.E.C. countries.

A significant feature of the Dutch labour market is the low rate of labour force participation. In the period 1960-79 the activity rate (ratio of labour force to population aged 15-64) fell from 59.2 to 57.1 per cent. It is well below that in other advanced capitalist countries, mainly because of very low female participation (which is however rising), but also because male participation (which is falling rapidly) is now lower than in other countries.

The main reason for the decline in male activity is the increased opportunity for non-work income which is more readily available than in other countries through the WAO scheme whereby people who acquire "handicapped" status receive 80 per cent of their former pay (indexed) until retirement age. It is sometimes assumed that a fraction of these former workers are unemployed, but people in this situation are most unlikely to return to the labour force unless their benefits are squeezed. The reasons for the low female activity rates are much more mysterious and have never been satisfactorily explained.

Another related phenomenon is the high incidence of "sickness" absence which occurs much more readily than in the past because social security now reduces the income loss. Table 3 shows that the incidence of such absence is more marked in the Netherlands than elsewhere.

Table 1
Unemployment as a Percent of the Labour Force

	Belgium	Denmark	France	Germany	Netherlands	U.K.	U.S.A.
1960–73	2.1	1.3	1.9	0.8	1.9	2.9	4.9
1974–79	5.4	4.9	4.5	3.6	5.9	4.9	6.8
1980	7.7	n.a.	6.3	3.3	7.8	9.4	7.1

Source : A. Maddison, Phases of Capitalist Development, Oxford University Press, 1982, and Annex 1 to this paper.

Table 2
Ratio of Labour Force to Population Aged 15-64, 1960-79

	Belgium	Denmark	France	Germany	Netherlands	U.K.	U.S.A.
MALES							
1960	88.5	99.5	92.6	94.1	92.8	98.7	91.7
1979	81.2	90.2	83.2	82.5	79.0	90.0	85.6
FEMALES							
1960	36.2	43.5	47.0	48.7	26.3	47.0	42.6
1979	47.5	71.6	52.5	49.2	34.7	57.8	58.9

Source : O.E.C.D., Labour Force Statistics, and Netherlands from Annex 1 to this paper.

Table 3
Working Days Lost Per Year Per Employee Through Compensated Sickness Absence

	France	Germany	Netherlands	U.K.
1960	13.2	13.9	10.4	13.8
1978	13.6	12.5	20.0	18.7

Source : A. Maddison, "Monitoring the Labour Market", Review of Income and Wealth, June 1980 and Annex 1 to this paper.

Table 4
Level of Productivity and Per Capita Income in 1979

	GDP per Man Hour	GDP per Head of Population	Employed as Proportion of Population	Annual Hours Worked Per Employed Person per Year	Annual Hours Worked per Head of Population
	U.S. = 100				
Belgium	88	82	39.0	1747	681
Denmark	64	74	49.4	1721	850
France	86	82	40.6	1727	701
Germany	84	82	41.5	1719	713
Netherlands	90	73	35.3	1679	593
U.K.	66	66	44.9	1617	726
U.S.A.	100	100	45.5	1607	731

Source : As for table 1.

As with the "handicapped" worker phenomenon, sickness absenteeism may be regarded as cushion mitigating unemployment, but there is no evidence that it is cyclical, nor that it would be reversed by an upturn in economic activity.

One important result of the low labour input in the Netherlands is that per capita real income is a good deal lower than the relative productivity performance of the country would suggest. Thus per capita real income in 1979 was at Danish levels though productivity was 40 per cent higher than in Denmark (see table 4).

The Dutch Conjuncture

Dutch economic growth slowed down markedly after 1973 to less than half the pace maintained in the golden age of 1960–73. This reflected the two recessions of 1975 and 1981 and faltering growth between these years. As can be seen from table 5, Dutch performance was not the worst, but growth was slower than in France and Germany.

Since 1973, the pace of inflation has accelerated in all countries, but the Netherlands has had less inflation than all other E.E.C. countries except Germany.

If one looks at the foreign balance, the Dutch situation has been exceptional with an average surplus as high in 1974–81 as in 1960–73.

Table 7 shows how the different components of demand have

changed since 1973 and compares these developments with the situation that prevailed in 1960-73. The most marked deceleration was in fixed investment and in exports, with export growth declining more markedly than in the other countries. Government consumption was sustained after 1973 at the same pace as in 1960-73.

Dutch policy since the OPEC shock and the world recession and slowdown of the 1970s has been cautious. Very high priority has been given to braking the pace of inflation and to remaining in the fixed exchange rate club (the snake, then EMS). Dutch success has been remarkable in terms of governmental objectives. The inflation rate was relatively modest, the payments surplus was maintained, and the exchange reserves (being heavily into gold) rose more in the 1970s than did world prices.

Table 5
Growth of GDP 1960-81

annual average compound growth rates

	1960-73	1973-81	1974	1975	1976
Belgium	5.0	1.9	4.5	-1.9	5.3
Denmark	4.6	1.5	-0.9	-0.6	7.9
France	5.6	2.7	3.2	0.2	5.2
Germany	4.5	2.0	0.5	-1.8	5.1
Netherlands	5.0	1.9	3.5	-1.0	5.3
U.K.	3.1	0.4	-1.2	-0.8	4.2
U.S.A.	4.0	1.9	-1.3	-1.0	5.6

annual average compound growth rates

	1977	1978	1979	1980	1981
Belgium	0.8	3.0	2.4	1.4	-0.5
Denmark	1.8	1.3	3.5	-1.0	0.0
France	2.8	3.6	3.1	1.3	-0.5
Germany	3.0	3.3	4.6	1.8	-1.5
Netherlands	2.4	2.5	2.2	0.8	-0.5
U.K.	1.0	3.6	0.9	-1.8	-1.5
U.S.A.	5.1	4.4	2.4	-0.2	2.5

Source : O.E.C.D., National Accounts of O.E.C.D. Countries and O.E.C.D. Economic Outlook, July 1981.

Table 6
Price and Payments Performance

	Rate of Change of Consumer Price Index		Current Balance of Payments as Percent of GDP (annual averages)	
	1960-73	1973-80	1960-73	1974-81
Belgium	3.6	8.2	1.0	-1.3
Denmark	6.2	11.1	-1.9	-2.7
France	4.5	11.1	0.3	-0.8
Germany	3.4	4.8	0.7	0.2
Netherlands	4.9	7.1	0.7	0.6
U.K.	5.1	15.8	-0.2	-0.5
U.S.A.	4.0	8.9	0.1	0.1

Source : O.E.C.D., Main Economic Indicators, and Economic Outlook, July 1981

Table 7
Movement in Volume of Demand by Main Expenditure Categories 1960-81

annual average compound growth rates

	Gross Fixed Capital Formation		Private Final Consumption	
	1960-73	1973-81	1960-73	1973-81
France	7.6	1.3	5.6	3.3
Germany	4.4	1.2	4.7	2.5
Netherlands	5.6	-0.5	5.6	2.3
U.K.	4.6	-1.6	2.8	0.9
U.S.A.	4.5[a]	-0.3[a]	4.2	2.5
Average	6.5	0.4	5.4	2.5

	Export of Goods and Services		Government Consumption	
	1960-73	1973-81	1960-73	1973-81
France	9.4	5.2	3.9	3.2
Germany	7.9	3.6	4.7	2.7
Netherlands	9.1	2.6	2.8	2.8
U.K.	5.1	2.3	2.5	2.0
U.S.A.	6.7	4.0	2.8	2.0
Average	8.9	4.9	3.8	2.7

a) excludes government capital formation.
Source : O.E.C.D., National Accounts of O.E.C.D. Countries, and Quarterly National Accounts Bulletin, 1980, (iv), 1981 forecasts from O.E.C.D., Economic Outlook, July 1981.

In facing the problems of the 1970s, the Dutch economy had three advantages (a) its 1973 boom was not excessive; (b) its new natural gas resources had already come on stream by the time of the OPEC shock, the country was more or less self sufficient in energy on a net basis, so its terms of trade and balance of payments were not hurt; (c) it had a more solidaristic social atmosphere, which made it much easier to maintain restraint in wage claims than in countries like France and the U.K. where social conflict is more acute.

The fiscal stance (the net result of automatic and discretionary action) was expansionist in 1974 and 1975, deflationary in 1976 and 1977 with some expansion in 1978 and 1979. Given the modest pace of inflation and the strong external position, it would seem that fiscal policy was overcautious in the first years after the OPEC shock.

Table 9 provides a crude indication of the monetary policy stance which was amongst the tightest of the countries shown. Over 1974-80 as a whole the real rate of interest was similar to that in Germany but there were bigger oscillations in the Netherlands. Since 1977 the Netherlands has had substantially higher real interest rates than Germany.

Table 8
Fiscal Stance : Government Net Lending as a Proportion of GDP
at Current Prices

	1973	1974	1975	1976	1977	1978	1979
France	0.9	0.6	-2.2	-0.5	-0.8	-1.8	-0.8
Germany	1.2	-1.4	-5.8	-3.6	-2.4	-2.8	-3.0
Netherlands	1.1	-0.1	-2.7	-2.4	-1.4	-2.2	-3.1
U.K.	-3.5	-3.8	-4.9	-5.0	-3.4	-4.3	-3.3
U.S.A.	1.0	0.5	-3.5	-1.5	-1.0	0.0	0.5

Source : Derived from National Accounts of O.E.C.D. Countries 1962-1979, Vol. II, O.E.C.D., Paris, 1981.

Table 9
Monetary Stance : Real Rate of Interest
(Discount Rate Divided by Consumer Price Increase)

	Average 1974-80	1974	1975	1976	1977	1978	1979	1980
France	-1.0	0.7	-3.8	0.9	0.1	-0.4	-1.3	-4.1
Germany	-0.1	-1.0	-2.5	-1.0	-0.7	0.3	1.9	2.0
Netherlands	-0.1	-2.6	-5.7	-2.8	1.9	1.4	5.3	1.5
U.K.	-3.5	--4.5	-13.5	-2.2	-8.9	4.2	3.6	-4.0
U.S.A.	-0.8	-3.3	-3.1	-0.6	-0.5	1.8	0.7	-0.5

Source : Discount rates end of period, from I.M.F. International Financial Statistics, prices from O.E.C.D. Main Economic Indicators.

Basic Characteristics of the Dutch Situation

(a) Openness

The Dutch economy is more open than most with a foreign trade ratio equal to about half of GDP, and no exchange controls for residents. Hence one would expect its foreign balance and employment position to be extremely sensitive to the exchange rate.

In spite of this the Netherlands has rejected exchange rate flexibility as a policy instrument, even though the guilder appreciated throughout the 1970s against all its main trading partners except the D Mark. This attitude is usually justified by the argument that wages are generally indexed and that improvements in the competitive position would be nullified by compensating wage increases. But the offset is unlikely to be complete and in such a pragmatic country, exceptions to the indexation rule can be made in exceptional circumstances (e.g. as in the case of professorial salaries). Exchange rate changes would also have an impact on the capital account. There may be other reasons why the allegiance to the D Mark is so strong, e.g. the benefits which the Netherlands receives from the E.E.C. agriculture policies which tend to be called in question by parity changes, or the potential for large destabilising foreign capital flows if the rate were not fixed. However, it is somewhat surprising to a foreign observer that there is not more discussion of this option in the Netherlands.

(b) The Welfare State

The Netherlands has a higher ratio of transfer payments than any other country and a level of total government spending second only to that of Sweden. This spending took a major leap in the 1960s under the influence of expected government revenues from natural gas, and has expanded further in the 1970s.

As a result, the Netherlands does not appear to have a poverty problem of the type so often discussied in the U.K., and as most social security benefits are taxed it does not have so many notches in the tax/transfer incidence (poverty traps) as many other countries. The pervasive nature of social security has given the Netherlands a sense of social solidarity and cohesion, and is not widely criticised in the Netherlands. The long run consequences of the system do seem to cause some disquiet, but the equity and efficiency problems have not been subject to very sophisticated analysis[1]. The various

components of government spending are usually lumped together
in what is vaguely called the collective sector, and the
government austerity programma (Bestek 81, p. 79) blithely
projects a rise in the number of handicapped people receiving
80 per cent of their previous income from 338,000 in 1975 to
660,000 in 1990.

(c)   Deindustrialisation

     A good deal of concern is felt in the Netherlands about
the decline of the industrial sector. The change in sectoral
structure is a long standing feature as in other countries, and
the industrial sector has been hit particularly hard by the
slowdown in growth since 1973. But the Dutch problem has been
complicated because the exploitation of natural gas has
strengthened the guilder and weakened the competitive position
of industry. In the U.K. this is known as the Dutch disease .
Government has tried to offset it by rather extensive subsidies
to industry. The success of such a policy depends on whether
the government makes sensible choices. The obvious alternative
to this selective interventionism is a more expansionist
macropolicy, with lower corporate taxes and a lower exchange
rate as a general stimulus to those industries with competitive
strength.

(d) Profits Squeeze

     There is great concern in the Netherlands with the squeeze
on profits over the last few years. This is a major point in
the papers by Kuipers and Kessler for this conference and it
figures prominently in most Dutch offical publications on the
conjunctural or medium term situation. It is also a point to
which central bankers and Marxists (see Harrison's
contribution) attach equal importance.
     The official discussion is usually conducted in terms of
the AIQ (arbeidsinkomenquote) which purports to show the labour
share of enterprise income after excluding depreciation and a
questionable adjustment to split the income of the self
employed into profit and labour income. This measure showed
profits to be a mere 6.2 per cent of income so defined in 1975.
But for the same year a careful O.E.C.D. study showed the gross
operating surplus to be 35.8 per cent of value added in
manufacturing, and the net operating surplus to be 29.5 per
cent. The O.E.C.D. figure shows higher profits in the
Netherlands than in other countries, and the net profit ratio

four times as high as that in the U.K.[2]].

Although government statistics on this important matter are exaggeratedly gloomy, it would not be surprising if profits were squeezed in a situation of recession and below-potential growth, particularly in a country highly dependent on exports whose exchange rate has appreciated.

The chosen policy option for remedying the situation is a long drawn out process of moderate wage growth to help profits. If the situation is as bleak as painted, quicker options seem preferable. However, the basic facts of the situation would seem to be worth more refined analysis, including a statement of the trend in gross profits including depreciation which will not have fallen so sharply, the situation gross and net of taxes and subsidies (the government now subsidizes employers' social security contributions), and the situation after allowance for price changes (as in the Scott's paper for this conference).

(e) Shortage of Capacity

It is suggested not infrequently in the Netherlands that in spite of sizeable unemployment, the economy is in fact working to capacity. This argument is sometimes on Hartog-Tjan grounds, i.e. it is alleged that so much capital has been scrapped because of high wages, that there is only enough to provide for those at present employed, and Kessler, who also makes this point in extremely strong form, bases it on the argument that there has been a virtual cessation of growth in productive capacity. I regard this argument as implausible whichever justification is used. There are no official estimates of capital stock in the Netherlands, but it is not difficult to construct rough estimates by a perpetual inventory technique similar to that used for other countries. These are shown in table 10 which shows a distinct slowing in the growth of capacity since 1973 but certainly not complete stagnation.

(f) Natural Gas Resources

In the 1970s the Dutch economy benefitted from the availability of natural gas from the Groningen area. At current rates of production (which have declined since 1976) the Netherlands has no net dependence on foreign energy. Its domestic output represented about 6.4 per cent of GDP in 1979, compared with 2.7 per cent in 1973. In 1979, North sea oil and gas represented about 4.7 per cent of British GDP, but the U.K.

share is rising (6.7 per cent in 1980, and likely to peak at around 10 per cent of GDP in 1985 [3]. A bigger proportion of the product goes to government revenue in the Netherlands than in the U.K., and none goes abroad in royalties to foreign companies. Revenue from gas resources has been smaller than it might have been both because the extraction rate was kept at a cautious level after 1976 and there has been some underpricing both in the domestic and export market. Here again we find a bias in policy which has hindered economic expansion.

Table 10

Growth of Gross Non Residential Fixed Capital Stock

annual average compound growth rates

	Growth of Stock		Growth of Stock Per Man Hour Employed	
	1960-73	1973-79	1960-73	1973-79
		a		a
France	5.1	4.7	5.1	5.2
Germany	6.2	4.3	7.0	6.0
Netherlands	6.9	4.6	7.2	5.2
U.K.	4.0	3.2	4.6	4.0
U.S.A.	4.0	3.3	2.6	2.0

a) 1973-78

Sources : France from INSEE; Germany from Volkswirtschaftliche Gesamtrechnungen, Statistical Office, Wiesbaden; U.K. supplied by Central Statistical Office; U.S.A. from Survey of Current Business, February 1981. Netherlands estimates as shown in annex 2.

Dutch Policy and Analysis

The Dutch economy was created and maintained by conquest of nature and intense preoccupation with hydraulic management. As a result of their success in basic physical engineering, the Dutch are also social engineers, treat socio-economic problems more technocratically than most countries, take pragmatic decisions without great trauma, and have a strong commitment to maintaining social order. Though political power is apparently fragmented into many parties, the bureaucratic decision-making process achieves a high degree of consensus because of its innate legitimacy and its technique of defusing criticism by a tentacular structure of advisory committees. Hence extreme divergencies of view are avoided, and eclecticism is common. Chauvinism and insularity are practically unknown, so policies which challenge the virtues of a liberal international order get no hearing. Partly because of the engineering bent, partly because of the non-literary character of Dutch education, Dutch economists communicate with each other for a good deal of the time via complex models, even though the basic data are often shaky. As a result, it is difficult to pin labels on Dutch policy and analysis which correspond to viewpoints, e.g. in the U.S.A. or U.K.

At first sight, the general Dutch policy posture in face of accelerated inflation and the slowdown in world growth since 1973 seems similar to that in many Western capitalist countries, and close to the revisionist Keynesianism advocated in the O.E.C.D.'s McCracken report[4]. This involved a mild counter-cyclical fiscal posture but with deliberate maintenance of demand below potential output in order to mitigate pressures on prices and the balance of payments. In the Netherlands this was accompanied by the functional equivalent of an incomes policy, though it is not described as such domestically. As in many countries, expenditure on labour market policy measures was stepped up and there were increased subsidies to industry.

The 1970s did not involve a sudden Dutch conversion to monetarist idiom. Unlike the U.K. and the U.S.A., the Netherlands had not rejected monetary policy in the 1950s, and there was hence no need to make the point that money matters in the 1970s[5]. Similarly there seems little tendency in the Netherlands to suggest that fiscal policy is impotent. The Dutch approach is properly characterised by Kessler as moderately monetarist.

In fact, official Dutch doctrine does not accept that the 1970s unemployment level was a deliberate sacrifice to attain other goals. A central thesis of government policy is the argument of the Central Planning Bureau that excessive wage claims over a long period have forced entrepreneurs to scrap old equipment, so that there is a shortage of capital. The argument goes further than the idea that wages are too high, because even if wages came down, there is supposed to be no suitable capital available to provide extra employment. In spite of a good deal of criticism, and the fact that the realism of several critical assumptions cannot be tested empirically[6], this line of argument has had wide appeal. Most participants seem to accept the implication that the wage share must be gradually whittled down and accept that business needs tax concessions and subsidies. Exchange rate depreciation is not advocated as a quicker route to higher profits. Presumably this is because of the deeply ingrained view that devaluation is impotent because of wage indexation, coupled with the belief that there is in any case no capacity to provide increased exports. There is also a tendency to argue that even if there were improved profits because of a depreciated exchange rate, the multinational companies which figure so largely in Dutch industry, would merely invest their increased profits in developing countries with low labour costs.

Because of the popularity of the Hartog-Tjan diagnosis, there are few Keynesian pundits advocating a government stimulus to demand in order to mitigate unemployment. Most of those who disagree with the Hartog-Tjan line and its policy implications[7] do not end up with proposals for general demand expansion, but for sectoral intervention to influence the pattern of investment and employment. Thus members of this group have some affinity in their thinking with the Cambridge Economic Policy Group in the U.K., but they do not push their analysis as far, mainly because explicit advocacy of protectionism is tabu in the Netherlands.

When one does catch a cryptic whiff of Keynesian argumentation in the Dutch discussion, it always seems to involve suggestions for increased public spending rather than tax reduction.

Another basic reason why Dutch Keynesianism is insignificant is that there was something of a cultural revolution in the late 1960s. The neo-bohemian, Mishan-Meadows attitudes towards economic growth are deeply entrenched in the Dutch intelligentsia. For many people, GNP growth is unimportant. Kessler makes a typical point in his paper for this conference when he says "a certain (preferably high) rate of economic growth no longer forms a generally accepted policy aim".

There is some discussion in the Netherlands of the increase in search unemployment in the 1970s compared with earlier years. Kessler refers to this in his paper as a "defective functioning of the labour market" and Kuipers calls it "worse functioning". The O.E.C.D. Economic Survey (March

1980) takes a similar view. Kuipers cites his own study of this phenomenon and that of Driehuis who obtained similar results. Kuipers suggests that this phenomenon accounts for 2.2 points of Dutch unemployment. It is not clear to me whether the suggestion is that there has been a net increase in the unemployment rate in the 1970s of this amount or whether the same phenomenon existed on a smaller scale in the 1950s and 1960s.

Both Kuipers and Driehuis derive their estimates by UV analysis, and I have not seen any Dutch work of the kind so popular in the U.K. and the U.S.A., and well represented by Nickell's article cited in Scott's paper. Here the central theme is the impact of changes in the unemployment benefit wage ratio on job search. Scott concludes that the U.K. unemployment rate rose by 1 point in the 1970s because of increases in frictional (job search) unemployment. My hunch is that this may be the underlying cause of what Kuipers and Driehius have detected in the Netherlands, but I would not consider it to be a defect in the functioning of the labour market, and I also feel that a good deal more work is needed before we can reach any firm conclusion about the magnitude of this phenomenon.

Apart from the current unemployment issue, there are a number of longer term problems of employment. One of these is the issue of de-industrialisation (already mentioned), another is the large size of employment in bureaucracy and government services (which is already a quarter of the labour force), a third is the likelihood on present policies, of a continuing increase in the number of non-active "handicapped" ex-workers, a fourth is the lack of job opportunities for women. Finally there is the situation which will arise when the gas runs out. When this happens the government will have to replace gas revenues by taxes or trim its expenditure, and in either case there will be difficult problems of incentives and adjustment. The high likelihood of these forthcoming problems in supply-side economics should condition the types of remedy used to tackle the current unemployment situation.

On my diagnosis, the following package of remedies for the Dutch employment situation suggests itself;

(i)   lower interest rates and taxes to promote economic expansion and fuller employment;

(ii)   a more formal incomes policy, in which more jobs and real income are offered in return for restraint in nominal wage claims;

(iii) a floating guilder;

(iv)   reductions in industrial subsidies and simplification of the tax structure to reduce tax exemptions;

(v)   erosion of those social benefits which cause reduction in labour supply, particularly handicapped and sickness benefits;

(vi)   government policies to encourage Scandinavian type labour force participation rates, i.e. more jobs for women and the handicapped;

(vii) conversion of a substantial proportion of public sector jobs to a part-time basis, both as a job creation measure and to increase efficiency by creating more competition for a smaller number of full time jobs;

(viii) improved basic statistics on the labour market, profits, capital stock, etc.

Notes

[1] e.g. S.E.R. Advies inzake omvang en groei van de collectieve sector, September 1978 which is an official review of trends and their causes in this area, is weaker analytically than the four O.E.C.D. reports on this problem, published between 1976 and 1978.

[2] For the AIQ, see Centraal Economisch Plan, CPB, The Hague, 1979, p. 329. For the O.E.C.D. figures, see T.P. Hill, Profits and Rates of Return, O.E.C.D., Paris, 1979, pp. 122-3. For a critique of the AIQ, see W. Salverda, Haalt de Arbeidsinkomens Quote de 100 Procent: (en wat dan nog) Tijdschrift voor Politieke Ekonomie, February 1978 (1977 : 4).

[3] Estimates derived from Kuiper's paper for this conference and from National Institute Economic Review, London, November 1979, p. 58.

[4] Towards Full Employment and Price Stability, O.E.C.D., Paris, June 1977.

[5] See H.G. Johnson, Inflation and The Monetarist Controversy, North Holland, Amsterdam, 1972, pp. 2-3. The Netherlands Bank maintained a serious, scholarly and practical interest in the monetary approach to the theory of economic stabilisation throughout a long period during which the Anglo-Saxon tradition in economics — has denigrated and dismissed the long-established insights of the monetary approach — what appear — as bold new monnetarist theories are essentially nearly identical with the commonplace precepts of Dutch monetary theory .

[6] See H. den Hartog and H.S. Tjan, Investments, Wages, Prices and Demand for Labour (A Clay-Clay Vintage Model for the Netherlands) , De Economist, 1976. This model makes two very extreme assumptions, a) that the rate of growth of labour saving technical progress quadrupled after 1947, and b) that it grew at 5.1 per cent a year thereafter. My own view on a) is that technical progress has probably not accelerated in the postwar period, given the lack of acceleration of productivity growth in the U.S.A. (which is the productivity leader). The pace of improvement assumed for post 1948 vintages is also implausibly high, for reasons advanced by Denison in critique of Solow, see E.F. Denison, Why growth

Rates Differ, Brookings, Washington D.C., 1967, chapter 12. The only country whose official capital stock estimates are adjusted for falling lengths of life of assets is Germany, and the changes assumed there are much less drastic than those assumed by Hartog and Tjan, see H. Lützel, "Estimates of Capital Stock by Industries in the Federal Republic of Germany", Review of Income and Wealth, March 1977.

[7] e.g. R.A. de Klerk, H.B.M. van der Laan, and K.B.T. Thio, "Unemployment in the Netherlands : a Criticism of the den Hartog-Tjan Vintage Model", Cambridge Journal of Economics, 1977. Driehuis appears to have similar views, but he is more academic, in that he usually advocates more research rather than specific policies in his conclusions.

ANNEX I

QUANTITATIVE CHANGES IN DUTCH LABOUR INPUTS 1960-1979

Labour Force Activity Rates and Population or Working Age

Traditionally Dutch estimates of the labour force have been presented annually in Nationale Rekeningen in terms of man years. The figures include the registered unemployed and people working on make-work projects. The method used to produce these estimates was last described in Arbeidsvolume en Geregistreerde Arbeidsreserve 1947-1966, CBS, 1967, from which it is clear that the figures do not correspond to man-year units in any normal sense, i.e. there is no adjustment for differences in hours worked by males and females, but merely for differences in the number of Sundays per year, and for sickness absence and accidents. Thus the Netherlands is the only country in the OECD Labour Force Statistics with no breakdown of the labour force by sex.

Since 1973 a labour force sample survey has been taken every two years, and these permit construction of the estimates in table 11. They refer to persons (not man-year equivalents) and are for mid-year. They are essentially the same in concept as those published by CBS in Sociale Maandstatistiek, September 1978, pp. 808-14 for 1971-78 for 1st January. A 1960 estimate was supplied by CBS.

Employment and Unemployment

The traditional unemployment figure includes only insured people with a financial incentive to register. The new sample survey figures have a wider catchment particularly for women. It is obvious from table 12 that the registration figures which are normally used as a labour market indicator are too low and need to be adjusted to a survey basis for purposes of international comparison. On a survey basis 1977 unemployment was 6 per cent of the labour force as compared with 4 per cent for the registration figures (i.e. taking the labour force estimate of table 11 as a denominator).

Working Time Per Person

Tables 14 and 15 were derived from Social Maandstatistiek and the Jaarverslag Arbeidsmarkt, both published by the Ministry of social Affairs, and the Labour Force Sample Surveys of Eurostat.

Table 11
Labour Force, Population of Working Age
and Activity Rates in the Netherlands, 1960-79

	Male Labour Force (All Ages) (000s)	Male Population Aged 15-64 (000s)	Male Activity Rate (per cent)	Female Labour Force (All Ages) (000s)
1960	3,222	3,471	92.8	930
1973	3,600	4,278	84.2	1,325
1974	3,605	4,337	83.1	1,362
1975	3,617	4,406	82.1	1,397
1976	3,630	4,476	81.1	1,433
1977	3,641	4,535	80.3	1,477
1978	3,655	4,596	79.5	1,525
1979	3,681	4,664	79.0	1,583

	Female Population Aged 15-64 (000s)	Female Activity Rate (per cent)	Total Labour Force (All Ages) (000s)	Total Population Aged 15-64 (000s)	Activity Rate (per cent)
1960	3,538	26.3	4.152	7.009	59.2
1973	4,207	31.5	4.925	8.485	58.0
1974	4,260	32.0	4.967	8.597	57.8
1975	4,322	32.3	5.014	8,728	57.4
1976	4,384	32.7	5,063	8,860	57.1
1977	4,442	33.3	5,118	8,977	57.0
1978	4,499	33.9	5,180	9,095	57.0
1979	4,560	34.7	5,264	9,224	57.1

Table 12
A Comparison of Registered Unemployment and LFSS Estimates of Unemployment

Registered Unemployed   Labour Force Sample Survey
Yearly average   March-May (thousands)
(thousands)

	Male	Female	Male	Female
1960	25.0	3.8		
1973	88.4	21.5	119.0	75.0
1974	106.7	28.2	n.a.	n.a.
1975	153.0	42.3	166.0	129.0
1976	159.8	51.0	n.a.	n.a.
1977	145.2	58.4	172.0	134.0
1978	136.4	69.2	n.a.	n.a.
1979	132.4	77.6	173.0	176.0
1980	159.1	88.0	n.a.	n.a.

Source : Registered figures from Tachtig Jaren Statistiek in Tijdreeksen, 1899-1979, CBS, 1979, p. 69. L.F.S.S. figures from Sociale Maandstatistiek, April and June 1975 (for 1973); Arbeidskrachtentelling 1975, CBS, 1978, (for 1975); Labour Force Sample Survey, 1977 and 1979 editions, Eurostat, Luxembourg, 1979 and 1981.

Table 13
Estimated Unemployment and Employment 1960-1978, not broken down by sex

	Registered Unemployment thousands	Estimated Unemployment adjusted to L.F.S.S. definitions thousands	Estimated Unemployment as Percent of Labour Force	Estimated Employment thousands
1960	28.8	50.8	1.2	4,101
1973	109.9	194.0	3.9	4,731
1974	134,9	221.0	4.4	4,746
1975	195.3	295.0	5.9	4,719
1976	210.8	318.0	6.3	4,745
1977	203.6	306.0	6.0	4,812
1978	205.6	323.3	6.2	4,857
1979	210.0	349.0	6.6	4,915

Table 14

Average Allocation of Days Per Year
Per Employee in the Netherlands 1960-79

	Total Days Per Year	Saturdays & Sundays	Public Holidays	Days of Vacation	Days of Incapacity
1960	366	105	6	13.0	10.4
1973	365	104	6	19.5	17.0
1974	365	104	6	20.0	18.0
1975	365	104	6	20.5	17.6
1976	366	104	6	21.0	18.6
1977	365	105	6	21.5	19.0
1978	365	105	6	22.0	20.0
1979	365	104	6	22.5	20.0

	Days Lost for Bad Weather, for Personal Reasons, & Industrial Disputes	Days Worked per Year
1960	1.0	230.6
1973	1.0	217.5
1974	1.0	216.0
1975	1.0	215.9
1976	1.0	215.4
1977	1.0	212.5
1978	1.0	211.0
1979	1.0	211.5

Table 15

Hours Worked Per Person in the Netherlands 1960-79

	Basic Weekly Hours of Full Time Workers	Impact of Part-time Workers Hours on Average Weekly Hours Worked	Weekly Overtime Hours	Average Weekly Short-Time Hours	Average Weekly Hours Worked Per Employee	Average Hours Worked Per Employee Per Day
1960	47.1	-0.6	0.70	-0.02	47.18	9.44
1973	42.4	-1.1	0.70	-0.05	41.95	8.39
1974	41.7	-1.2	0.43	-0.20	40.73	8.15
1975	40.9	-1.3	0.43	-0.79	39.24	7.85
1976	40.9	-1.3	0.43	-0.35	39.68	7.94
1977	40.7	-1.3	0.43	-0.27	39.56	7.91
1978	40.6	-1.3	0.43	-0.13	39.60	7.92
1979	40.6	-1.3	0.43	-0.03	39.70	7.94

ANNEX 2

DERIVATION OF ESTIMATES OF DUTCH GROSS NON RESIDENTIAL FIXED
CAPITAL STOCK

The estimates in table 10 were derived from table 16, by
the perpetual inventory technique, assuming all assets have a
life of 30 years. Thus the capital stock in midyear 1960 is
derived by cumulating the increments in capital stock from mid
1930 to mid 1960, i.e. the 1931-59 increments and half the 1930
and 1960 increments. A 15 per cent reduction to the 1930-43
increments was applied in order to allow for war damage.

GDP for 1950 onwards from National Accounts of OECD
Countries, various editions; for earlier years the movement was
assumed to parallel that for net domestic product in Zestig
Jaren Statistiek in Tijdreeksen, CBS, 1959, p. 102, except for
1939-47 which was derived from real product in international
units in C. Clark, Conditions of Economic Progress, Macmillan,
London, 1957, pp. 166-7.

Ratios of investment to GDP for 1950 onwards from OECD,
Op. cit. For 1930-50, it was assumed that non-residential
investment as a whole moved as did machinery and equipment
investment in enterprises, as shown by H. den Hartog and H.S.
Tjan "A Clay-Clay Vintage Model Approach for Sectors of
Industry in the Netherlands", CPB, The Hague, September 1979,
Appendix 7.
The increments (expressed as a percentage of 1950 GDP) are
derived by multiplying the GDP index and the investment ratio
for the corresponding year.

Table 16

Derivation of Capital Stock

	GDP (1950=100)	Ratio of Gross Fixed Non-Residential Capital Formation to GDP	Gross Increment to Capital Stock (as Percentage of 1950 GDP
1930	69.2	17.7	12.3
1931	66.9	13.0	8.7
1932	64.6	8.2	5.3
1933	62.9	9.2	5.8
1934	63.5	9.1	5.8
1935	65.1	7.6	5.0
1936	66.4	8.4	5.6
1937	70.0	10.7	7.5
1938	70.6	13.0	9.2
1939	73.3	13.8	10.1
1940	65.8	8.6	5.7
1941	67.0	6.1	4.1
1942	61.2	3.8	2.3
1943	59.5	3.1	1.8
1944	40.2	0.0	0.0
1945	40.8	0.0	0.0
1946	71.3	7.1	5.1
1947	82.3	13.2	10.8
1948	91.1	14.8	13.5
1949	96.9	15.1	14.6
1950	100.0	16.4	16.4
1951	101.8	15.9	16.2
1952	103.7	15.0	15.6
1953	112.3	16.8	18.9
1954	119.8	17.3	20.7
1955	128.2	19.1	24.5
1956	133.9	20.5	27.4
1957	137.9	20.5	28.3
1958	136.5	17.8	24.3
1959	143.0	18.8	26.9

Table 16

Derivation of Capital Stock

	GDP (1950=100)	Ratio of Gross Fixed Non-Residential Capital Formation to GDP	Gross Increment to Capital Stock (as Percentage of 1950 GDP	Mid-Year Gross Fixed Non-Residential Capital Stock (expressed as percentage of 1950 GDP)
1960	155.9	19.5	30.4	349.0
1961	160.7	20.3	32.6	
1962	167.0	20.4	34.1	
1963	173.1	19.8	34.3	
1964	187.4	20.6	38.6	
1965	197.2	20.0	39.4	
1966	203.5	20.8	42.3	
1967	213.4	20.6	44.0	
1968	227.1	21.0	47.7	
1969	241.6	19.1	46.1	
1970	257.9	20.4	52.6	
1971	268.9	20.0	53.8	
1972	278.1	17.3	48.1	
1973	293.9	16.7	49.1	832.5
1974	304.3	16.3	49.6	
1975	301.2	15.7	47.3	
1976	317.2	14.3	45.4	
1977	324.7	15.2	49.4	
1978	332.8	15.5	51.6	
1979	340.0	15.8	53.7	1,089.8

COMMENTS ON MADDISON'S PAPER

Jan Pen, University of Groningen

The paper is refreshing because of its international
perspective.   It takes a distant look at our national
proclivities and compares the data of the European family.
Maddison also wonders what has happened to the Dutch
Keynesians - a question dear to my heart.   The paper is
encouraging: it tells us that the performance of the Dutch
economy is not so bad.   Maddison even says "Dutch success has
been remarkable, in terms of governmental objectives".   That
is good news.

Unfortunately, the message is not quite convincing.   The
objectives of the Dutch government are at least threefold:
to decrease unemployment, to stabilize (or decrease) the tax
burden, and to restore profits.   None of these goals has been
achieved.   Moreover, the budgetary deficit and the deficit on
the balance of payments exceed the limits set by the cabinet.
So the question is: what are the objectives that Maddison
has in mind?   One could imagine that a government would say:
"we are satisfied if things at home are not going worse than
in the rest of Europe", but this stance has not been taken
officially.

The near-stable employment is due to the expansion of
the public sector.   This expansion was contrary to the aims
of Bestek '81, though it was in accordance with the views of
the Labour Party, which are perhaps a little bit more on the
Keynesian side.

The balance of payments is of course worse than meets
the eye;   if correction is made for (temporary) gas revenues
the deficit is at least 7 per cent of GNP.   This is actually
one of our principal worries and the biggest stumbling block
to a Keynesian policy.   Maddison seems to be slightly
surprised by the silence of the Dutch Keynesians but perhaps
the balance of payments gloom is the main explanation.

Maddison reproaches the domestic observers - mildly -
for not recommending tax cuts as an instrument of Keynesian
policy.   Here I agree with him in so far that this Keynesian
argument is hardly ever used to fight the trade union
position that wage moderation will reduce purchasing power
and therefore demand and employment.   This "purchasing power

argument" is old and well-known; we are reminded of discussions in the Weimar republic. A tax cut can work wonders to restore the purchasing power of the workers and one good reason for an incomes policy is that it opens the road to such a tax cut. But I disagree with Maddison when he suggests that tax reduction was never recommended to solve the employment problem. On the contrary: listening to the entrepreneurial vox populi one gets the impression that the main problem of the Dutch economy is uncut taxes. Unfortunately, we cannot reduce taxation because we have no confidence in our balance of payments and we are scared of the budgetary deficit.

A Keynesian policy is also rejected by some Dutch observers - among them the Central Planning Bureau - because they believe that there is hardly any slack capacity in the domestic market. Maddison looks at these commentators with a certain surprise and here I share his feelings. The slack is obviously there. Yet I must concede that it does not stay where it is. Plants are closed, machinery disappears, human skills are unlearned. Capacity is frittered away. If we do not conduct a Keynesian policy, its raison d'etre is destroyed by neglect. I offer this argument as an additional support for Maddison's view that an expansionary policy ought to be considered.

Maddison does not discuss the budgetary deficit as a brake on a Keynesian policy. His "net Government lending" table stops at 1979, at 3.1 per cent of GDP. However, the present figure is more than twice as high and acts as an additional constraint on tax cuts.[1] Apart from strong irrational fears there is the possibility of crowding out and higher rates of interest. And these high rates of interest are a threat to business. They further reduce the profitability of industry and they reduce net investments.

I feel that investment is lower than Maddison suggests. Gross figures are misleading in times of what is now called "accelerated scrapping". Whole chunks of industrial equipment are crumbling away. Net capital formation may well be zero. We live, for the time being, in a stagnating economy and Maddison's assertion to the contrary may be good for morale but it is not convincing.

That brings me to a point where I really disagree with Maddison and that concerns the profit squeeze. Maddison is critical of the statistical fashion in which the Dutch handle profits. He berates us for using the complement to the AIQ and rightly so; but he overlooks certain endeavours to estimate true profitability. Rents and interest on loans and perhaps on total capital should be deducted and depreciation should be taken into account. In passing, Maddison recommends Hill — who does not make these deductions and therefore figures that the Dutch "gross operating surplus" was 35.8 per cent of GDP in 1975. Then Maddison concludes from Hill's carefully presented comparative estimates' that profits were well sustained (until 1975!) — thus falling in the conceptual trap of confusing GOS with genuine profits. One of the differences between GOS and profits is interest — if the interest rate goes up, GOS increases but profits go down. Another difference is depreciation — when substantial parts of the capital stock are washed away, depreciation may be much higher than traditional methods will show. My own estimate of actual net profits in domestic manufacturing industry is that they were about zero in 1977, and negative in later years[2]].

Maddison reflects, in one fleeting sentence, on the possibility that the profit situation is indeed as bleak as it is painted, and he suggests that "quicker options" for the restoration of profitability are preferable. I fully agree with this, but the trouble is that the Dutch do not agree about the options. My own recommendations are the following. (a) A strict incomes policy, which means increases in the level of money incomes according to productivity. (b) A devaluation of the guilder. (c) Increases in the volume of public spending, financed by reductions in public salaries. (d) A nominal rate of interest of say 3 to 5 per cent. (e) Tax reductions to keep purchasing power at the right level and restore after-tax profits. But this policy package will be hit by a number of vetos from our well-organized interest groups. Veto power is the principal barrier to a new type of what Maddison might call "hydraulic management".

Notes

[1] In 1981, the budget deficit was 8 per cent of GDP. It led to some political trouble (cabinet crisis, etc.).

[2] See J. Pen, "Profits as a Rich Source of Puzzlement", De Economist, 128, No. 3, 1980, p. 285. For 1977, total profits were estimated at 8 per cent of national income. This is before tax. After tax the figure was less than 6 per cent. Half these profits stem from four (!) multinational corporations. Moreover, banks and insurance companies did well, which means that, at best, nothing was left for manufacturing industry. If interest on total capital is considered as a cost, there were losses – at least 5 per cent of national income. Since 1977, profitability has not improved.

DO KEYNESIAN DIAGNOSES AND REMEDIES NEED REVISION?

Deepak Lal,* World Bank and University College London

INTRODUCTION

The first part of this paper provides a critical survey of the recent rational expectations and implicit contract theories. The second attempts to provide a rationale for Keynesian type behaviour in industrial labour markets, in a world of irreducible uncertainty, moral hazard and firm-specific human capital. The third examines various policy dilemmas in the current stagflationary conjuncture; argues that constant money supply growth rate rules are not operational in the pure credit economies that are characteristic of most OECD countries and thence argues for reintroducing interest rate policy as the major instrument of monetary stabilisation. In this context the role of fiscalism in Keynesian economics is reconsidered, and it is argued that it may be desirable to concentrate on allocative and equity rather than stabilisation aspects in designing government budgets. Finally, we examine the implications of the absence of a world central bank for the international monetary system which is increasingly a pure credit system.

THE NEW CLASSICAL MACROECONOMICS AND IMPLICIT CONTRACT THEORY

It had long been recognised that the price-theoretic underpinnings of the General Theory were pretty weak. The Phillips curve type theory as propounded by Lipsey seemed to provide a theoretical underpinning to Phillips' statistical relationship, along which (in the grey zone where the aggregate supply curve in price output space was neither horizontal nor vertical) aggregate demand policy (monetary and/or fiscal) could tradeoff a reduced unemployment rate against an increased inflation rate.

Natural Rate of Unemployment Theories

The first major attack on this Keynesian position was provided by Friedman and Phelps. They argued that there is a

* The author is Reader in Policical Economy at University College London. The paper was written whilst he was on leave at the World Bank. The views expressed are personal and should not be attributed in any way to the World Bank or its affiliates.

natural rate of unemployment due to frictional and structural factors which cannot be reduced in the long run by raising aggregate demand, without an accelerating increase in the price level. Thus whilst in the short run there may be a negatively sloped Phillips curve due to the money illusion of workers, in the long run the Phillips curve is vertical.

On this natural rate hypothesis the authorities were able to "fool" workers with adaptive expectations, suffering from money illusion, in the short run. So that by generating an inflation rate greater than their expected rate (which was based on extrapolating the past), workers would implicitly be accepting a cut in real wages and hence employment would increase. However, in the long run, workers seeing that their real wages had been cut would demand and get a restoration of their old real wage, and return to the natural rate level of unemployment. Thus in the long run there would be a vertical Phillips curve.

Furthermore, any reduction in unemployment below the natural rate following a once-for-all increase in the inflation rate would soon be nullified as workers 'saw through' the cut in real wages that it entailed. To ensure the lower rate of unemployment it would be necessary for the authorities to generate an accelerating inflation which, because of the lag in the process of expectation formation, would continually fool workers to accept the required cut in real wages.

Rational Expectations

However, as was emphasized by Muth the above adaptive expectations formation process is irrational because, if workers have the same information, and make the same assumptions about the working of the economy as the government and its economic advisors, then they will immediately realise that, an increase in the money supply, implying more inflation, will mean a cut in their real wage. They will therefore correctly predict the future course of prices flowing from anticipated government policy and hence change the nominal prices under their control to maintain the existing (and unchanged) equilibrium real values. Hence, public policies to expand demand will lose their ability to hold the unemployment rate below the natural rate, even in the short run. Both the short and long run Phillips curves would be vertical. The difference between 'rational' price expectations and actual prices will be due entirely to forecasting error. So that, it is only by "surprise", that is by doing the unexpected that monetary policy can affect real variables such as the unemployment rate in the economy.

These are powerful results which have been extended and applied by numerous monetarist authors to illustrate both the impotency of any feedback type of monetary policy rule which they argue will be fully anticipated by 'rational' agents, as well as the desirability of the fixed money growth rule, advocated by Friedman (1968). (See Barro 1976, Lucas 1972, Sargent-Wallace 1975).

Two separate sets of issues are raised by this full scale and seemingly successful monetarist counter-attack on the Keynesian position. The first concerns the validity of the assumption of rational expectations. The second, whether even if the assumption of rational expectations is allowed, the policy conclusions about the short run neutrality of money follow. I will not deal with the latter in this paper as it seems pointless to consider outcomes in worlds with full-fledged rational expectations if, as I argue below, such a world is unlikely to be relevant for most industrial countries.

The intuitive power of the notion of rational expectations derives from its validity in a number of important real world markets — these are the well-organised markets for primary commodities, foreign exchange and common stocks. These markets are characterised by the "flexprice" features which have commonly been ascribed to all markets in the textbook Walrasian general equilibrium model. These organised markets, are markets which work by rules. The brokers are the key element in these organised markets (much as are the merchants and traders in the unorganised markets which still categorise most developing countries markets for goods). They lower or raise prices whenever profitable arbitrage is possible, and keep the markets atomistic. In such organised markets, moreover, at least when they are not impossibly "thin", participants are able to indulge in constant recontracting. This means that market participants can act on the basis of the latest available and continually changing information both about the real world, and the expectations of other market participants as revealed through their current actions, in determining the relevant spot (or future — if future markets exists) prices. In these markets, (partly because the market price also reveals the expectations of other markets participants), price adjustments to emerging information will be rapid and hence the information too will be rapidly disseminated. As such, behaviour on these flex price or auction markets will conform to the rational expectations hypothesis; the price changes in these markets will also reflect the characteristic of so-called efficient markets, that price changes on such markets follow an approximately random walk. The 'efficient' prices established on such markets will be equilibrium prices which are conditional on the available information when such prices are set. Furthermore, it will not be possible to improve the 'stability' of the prices set in these markets, given the underlying random walk nature of the fluctuations these prices reflect, unless there is an omniscient agent who can foretell the future better than current market participants. If such an agent (say the government) existed, he or she could make large profits in these markets at the expense of the other more ignorant participants. Hence public policy aimed at stabilising prices in these markets must imply that the government has access to 'better' information which enables it to profitably speculate in these markets. Even if this were so, it might be better for the government to disseminate its information, rather than profit from it at the expense of some of its citizens. But it is unlikely that governments have better information and that stabilising public speculation is likely to be either feasible or desirable.

The essential point therefore is that, if all markets in an economy were of the above flex-price kind in which the rational expectations hypothesis was valid, then the major conclusion on the impotency of stabilisation policies could be justified. However, the essential Keynesian insight is that in most industrial countries, apart from the organised markets listed above, most other markets and in particular the labour market are not flex price but rather fix price markets. That this is a Hicksian insight. Keynes muddied the water in his chapter on "Long Term Expectations" in the General Theory, where his peroration on the stock market has left the impression on innumerable readers that behaviour on it (and by implication on other organised markets) is irrational. Many have hence concluded that in the face of the irreducible uncertainty, so eloquently characterised by Keynes in this chapter and in his 1937 QJE article, behaviour on all markets is 'irrational' in the sense of not conforming to the postulates of rationality underlying the Walrasian general equilibrium construct.

The truth, as most often, is likely to lie between the extreme rational expectations hypothesis as applying to all markets as held by current monetarists, or none as seemingly advanced by Keynes and some of his followers. For our purposes, it is sufficient if reasons can be found why the rational expectations hypothesis may be inapplicable to labour but apply to primary commodity, foreign exchange and stock markets. For that would be sufficient to salvage the major Keynesian insights and remedies from the new classical counter-attack.

Implicit Contracts – A Successful 'Keynesian' Counterattack?

It maybe thought that, given the above distinction between the two sets of markets (in terms of fix versus flex price), providing good reasons for expecting the labour market in modern industrial countries to be a fix price rather than a flex price market, would be sufficient to contradict the policy conclusions flowing from the rational expectations hypothesis. The recent so-called "implicit contracts" theories (see Azariadis, Bailey, Gordon) are relevant in this context.

The essential insight of these theories is that, if workers are more risk averse than producers, who may have access to more perfect capital markets, then in the face of given demand fluctuations, it may be in the interests of producers to offer and workers to accept fixed wage contracts, as the latter provide an element of risk shifting (insurance) from the more risk averse workers to the less risk averse producers. Thus consider the following simple model. We assume that each firm has a pool of homogenous workers, all of whom can be employed when the firm is working at full capacity. However, there are random fluctuations in the demand (price) of the firm's output, which can be described by a probability distribution of expected outputs (prices) of the firm. This means that the value marginal product of labour (vmp) will be fluctuating over the cycle.

Now consider various alternative labour contracts. The first is the traditional spot contract, where all the workers are employed at a wage equal to their fluctuating (vmp). The utility level of risk averse workers (see Fig. 1) will then be given by the level $\bar{U}$, which corresponds to that associated with the expected wage w. They however, would be equally happy with the certainty equivalent lower fixed wage $\bar{w}$. An alternative fixed wage contract at wage $\bar{w}$ would also be preferred by risk neutral producers, whose average wage payment will then decline from the mean of the fluctuating vmp of w to $\bar{w}$. Thus it would be in the interests of both employers and employees to accept a fix wage contract, in which wages are fixed at the level $\bar{w}$ say, but employment fluctuates as in the case of the spot contract[1]. This could be taken to provide the underpinning for Keynesian type of employment fluctuations and an economic justification for both the ensuing wage-rigidity and Keynesian type policies to stabilise aggregate demand and hence employment.

However, as was soon perceived (see Barro 1977) and thereafter formalised (see Akerlof and Miyazaki), the above fixed wage variable employment contract though Pareto – superior to a variable wage employment contract is nevertheless Pareto – inferior to a fixed wage cum fixed employment contract. For in the previous case, risk averse workers would still have a finite probability of being laid off, when ex hypothesi their utility level would fall to zero (we discuss the difference that a positive reservation wage makes to the argument below). They would therefore accept a contract with a yet lower wage (lower than $\bar{w}$ but which guaranteed their employment in all states of nature, to the variable employment and fixed wage ($\bar{w}$) contract. Moreover, risk-neutral employers too would be willing to offer this contract as they are merely concerned with their total wage bill which would go down with the new lower wage - fixed employment contract[2]. Thus, even with demand uncertainty, and differing degrees of risk aversion between workers and employers, though wages would be rigid during the cycle, unlike the Keynesian case there would now be full employment at all times. Thus, as in the rational expectations model, we once again get automatic full employment assured, with a rigid wage (and long term contracts) even in this supposedly Keynesian type model!

This is not because of the simplifying assumptions that have hitherto been made, in particular that the effective utility function of workers is strictly concave over its whole range. It might be thought if there is a reservation wage (corresponding in Fig. 1, to a utility level Uo and wage level w_o) - or else an alternative income through unemployment insurance that as the effective utility function becomes non concave (Uo, U), fixed wages and fluctuating employment would again become the Pareto superior policy in the face of demand fluctuations. It can be readily shown (see Akerlof and Miyazaki) that as long as the utility and profit maximizing fixed wage associated with the fixed employment contract is greater than the reservation wage w_o , the former will still be adopted. Only if the fixed wage associated with full employment is less then w_o, will there be some variability in wages and lay offs and voluntary unemployment when the marginal product of labour falls below w_o. But this latter result offers no consolation to Keynesians, as the resulting unemployment is in essence no different from that arising in the alternative Walrasian, variable wage, spot - contracting case, when labour has a reservation wage. In fact the levels of such voluntary unemployment predicted by the implicit contract theory would be lower than those under spot contracting (see Akerlof and Miyazaki).

Irreducible Uncertainty and Keynesian Disequilibria - The Missing Battalion in the Keynesian Counter-attack

Thus whilst the implicit contract theory is of importance in explaining certain features of the structure of wages (and their relative rigidity) in industrial economies, within the traditional utility and profit maximising framework, it clearly cannot provide an explanation for Keynesian type cyclical unemployment. The reason why we have spent some time in spelling out this case is that it points to an important insight of Keynesian economics, which is missed by attempts at explaining Keynesian type unemployment within an 'equilibrium' framework, namely that Keynesian unemployment, as well as the trade cycles with which it is associated are a disequilibrium phenomenon in the sense that there are unexploited profit opportunities in a slump. This in turn as Keynes emphasised is due to the nature of the uncertainty that economic agents face, in particular when considering their investment decisions.

The implicit contracts theory is within the 'equilibrium' framework as it reduces all uncertainty to risk (in the Knightian sense). If this can be done (so that there is a rational basis for numerical probability estimates of the relative frequency kind to be assigned to states of nature) then the economy will most likely end up in a rational expectations equilibrium, without any Keynesian unemployment. This has been explicitly recognised by one of the progenitors of the rational expectations hypothesis in macroeconomics, Lucas, who writes :

> "Unfortunately, the general hypothesis that economic agents are Bayesian decision makers has, in many application little empirical content : without some way of inferring what an agent's subjective view of the future is, this hypothesis is of no help in understanding his behaviour... John Muth (1961) proposed to resolve this problem by identifying agents subjective probabilities with observed frequencies of the events to be forecast, or with "true" probabilities, calling the assumed coincidence of subjective and "true" probabilities rational expectations. Evidently, this hypothesis will not be of value in understanding psychotic behaviour. Neither will it be applicable in situations in which one cannot guess which if any, observable frequencies are relevant : situations which Knight called "uncertainty". It will most likely be useful in situations in which probabilities of interest concern a fairly well defined recurrent event, situations of "risk" in Knight's terminology. In situations of risk, the hypothesis of rationasl behaviour on the part of agents will have usable content, so that behaviour may be explainable in terms of economic

theory. In such situations, expectations are rational in Muth's sense. In cases of uncertainty, economic reasoning will be of no value". (Lucas 1977, p. 13).

But Keynes emphasised that the uncertainty which he thought lay at the heart of the processes explaining cyclical fluctuations (caused by the changing "animal spirits" of entrepreneurs) was the irreducible uncertainty of Knight's. Unfortunately, for most contemporary macroeconomists, "economic theorising" (Lucas) is the application of what Hicks (1979) has termed the static method to the problems of sequential causation — the form of causation, which must underlie explanations (and thence predictions) of genuine real-world dynamic processes, in which ignorance (and not mere risk) of the future forms an integral part, as emphasised by Keynes. Both stress that the static method cannot be used to reduce these processes into mechanical analogies from which macroeconometric models can be estimated. Moreover, if aspects concerning irreducible uncertainty are a major part of the explanation for trade cycles, it is surely illegitimate to ignore these aspects because the static method is thereby made unusable. Nor does it mean that economic theorising, which is not so narrowly identified with the application of the static method, need cease. Keynes and the later Hicks exemplify how, even if irreducible uncertainty is taken seriously, economic analysis can yield qualitative policy conclusions (which however must be rooted in the actual histories of particular economies).

As it is primarily labour market behaviour during the trade cycle which is of importance in the on-going debate between Keynesians and the New Classicals, it will be appropriate to sketch an outline of a simple economic model which builds on Keynesian insghts, those implicit in the implicit contracts theories, the later Hicks, and recent analyses of so-called 'dual' or internal labour markets.

A SKETCH OF THE KEYNESIAN PROCESS IN INDUSTRIAL LABOUR MARKETS

One of the essential building blocks for a Keynesian type outcome in industrial labour markets, is the recognition of the importance of firm specific training which converts labour into a quasi-fixed factor of production (see Oi). Thus labour, unlike many of the raw material inputs which all enter the firm's production process, ceases to be a purely variable input which can be hired and fired at will in an auction market.

Instead it is like the fixed physical capital of the firm, whose value depends (in part) upon the expected quasi rents (profits) that the firm hopes to recoup from the firm specific human capital embodied in its workers. The reason why this firm specific capital cannot be traded on auction markets, is that its existence creates the small number bargaining problem associated with bilateral monopoly; thus controverting the large numbers assumption required for the functioning of auction markets. For a worker with firm specific capital is from the viewpoint of the firm differentiated from other workers (with equivalent general skills). Whilst the worker's value to his present employer is greater than that to other employers.

The existence of this firm specific human capital entails a rental element in the cost of using labour services (as with machines) which will in part be inversely related to the time the firm can utilise this capital (for any given level of wages that are paid to the workers). The firm will thus have an incentive to "tie in" the worker to the firm, through various well known devices to reduce turnover and to lengthen the tenure of the worker. For the worker too, there is an incentive to stay with the firm as his alternative income in another firm will be lower as his value marginal product there will be lower (at least till he has received the specific training required in that firm). Moreover, for the type of risk-aversion reasons emphasised in the implicit contract theory discussed above, the worker and the employer will prefer some fixed wage - fixed employment contract given the 'rationally expected' fluctuations in future demand.

These 'rationally expected' fluctuations are the 'normal' fluctuations for which some kind of 'objective' numerical probabilities of the relative frequency type can be assigned, as in rational expectations models. In the face of this known risk we would expect fixed wage and employment contracts to be established. However, in addition the firm (as well as the workers) will be faced with the irreducible uncertainty that there may be unforseeable and hence unforeseen deviations from this normal "band". With irreducible uncertainty it can never be optimal for the firm to guarantee employment in every conceivable state of nature, for one of these unexpected states could be bankruptcy. The resulting contracts must then take account of this irreducible uncertainty to which no 'objective' and hence commonly agreed numerical probabilities can be attached.

A firm in this environment will be concerned with optimising the variable hours in the production process of its labourers. Its decision variables will be variations in hours per worker differentiated by 'types' of labour. Types of workers for whom the optimum hours of work from the firm's viewpoint are zero, will be laid off (either temporarily or permanently). As these decisions about variable hours will also determine the utility levels of workers, clearly the contracts will have to specify the hours worked per worker when demand for the firms product deviates from the 'normal' band.

If it were unambigously clear to workers when and to what extent demand had deviated from the "normal" band, they would once again as in the pure risk-type implicit contract theory, be willing to accept wage cuts with full employment, as long as the resulting wage was not less than their reservation wage (which includes any unemployment insurance benefits).

However, for much of the output of manufactured goods it will not be possible for workers to monitor these output changes accurately, and this in turn will entail problems of moral hazard on the part of producers. For most manufactured goods prices are 'fix price' and not 'flex price' because "normal" stock-holding of the relevant output can smooth 'normal' fluctuations in demand. This 'normal' level of stock-holding, depite the impression created by mechanical stock-adjustment rules built into mathematical models, is not by any means a technological datum (see Hicks 1965). Hence it will always be open to dispute whether or not a particular fluctuation in stocks represents a deviation from the 'normal' band. The moral hazard problem then is that the workers will rightly fear that employers might use a phony rise in stocks above what they claim is the normal level to force a general wage cut on its employees. The latter will therefore prefer an alternative form of contract in which this moral hazard on the part of producers is reduced. In such a contract (with the given fixed hours per worker), the workers would accept temporary (or permanent) layoffs when demand was unexpectedly below 'normal' but no cut in money wages. The fact that the firm was laying off workers would be a genuine signal that in fact "bad times were here again"!

What is more, given the different amounts of firm specific human capital embodied in its workers, there would be a clear profit maximising pattern to the layoffs. Assuming (unrealistically) some substitutability amongst the members of its work force, the workers with less firm specific human capital will be laid off first.

But given this pattern of layoffs which will be predictable, why should the workers with the least specific human capital not cut their wages when they are about to be laid off, thereby making it profitable for them to be employed by undercutting the wages of those with more specific human capital? If this were the case, we would again be back to full employment with all workers in the firm accepting the requisite wage cuts.

Keynes' important insight that, workers will accept a real wage reduction caused by a general rise in the price level, but will not accept the same result brought about by a cut in money wages, privides a hint. Because of the specific human capital of its workforce it is in the interests of both parties in the labour market to maintain a fair degree of permanency in their relationship. Thus, ceteris paribus workers will have joined a particular firm on the expectation that their long term prospects in it are at least as good as those of their peers with similar general skills, who have joined other firms. If the derived demand for their labour in the firm they have joined falls it will not be apparent to them whether this is a fall in the overall demand for the general skills they have, or merely for the firm specific human capital they have acquired. For their current value marginal product will reflect both the return to their general skill, whose value will depend upon the overall demand and supply for that skill, as well as their share in the increase in their marginal product (over and above that associated with the general skill) which has been made possible by the investment of the firm (or jointly by the worker and the firm) in their specific human capital. If they were certain that it was the demand for their general skill which had fallen, they might be willing to accept a wage cut. But what they observe (assuming they can) is a fall in the joint marginal product of their general and specific skills. At least part of the fall in the latter should be borne by the employer. The only way they can judge whether the fall in their value marginal product is due to a decline in demand for their general rather than specific skills, is if money wages cuts have been accepted by workers in comparable occupations, and with comparable degrees of seniority, in various other industries, which maybe taken as a crude surrogate of the amount of embodied firm specific capital.

This of course is just a special case of the more general argument that lacking a Walrasian auctioneer, it is difficult for workers to determine instantaneously whether or not the local fall in demand for their particular services is a general fall in the demand for that class of labour as a whole. Even the workers with little or no specific training will then not be willing to reduce their reservation money wage when they are laid off. For the general skills which they have are likely to

be embodied in a large section of the workforce, few of whom
will in fact be laid off, even during a recession. There will,
thus, be involuntary unemployment at the given money wage,
which could be 'cured' if the general price level and thence
the real (but not money) wages of all the workers with the same
general skills fell together.

Thus, workers may be concerned about relative real wage
differentials (in their money wage bargaining) not merely
because, as is traditionally argued, relative wages (because of
envy) are an argument in their utility functions, but because
such comparisons are an important signal when workers cannot
accurately assess whether the fall in the local demand for
their services (in the firm to which they are attached) is an
overall decline in the value marginal product of their general
or merely their firm-specific human capital.

The above sketch shows how in labour markets where firm
specific human capital is of importance and irreducible
uncertainty is pervasive, fix price labour market behaviour
with the observed Keynesian type cyclical movements of
employment in the face of changing aggregate demand may be
observed.

Furthermore, once the importance (and rationality) of
these relative wage comparisons is allowed in the labour
markets of industrial countries, then the lack of an economy
wide auctioneer or co-ordinator to call out the 'equilibrium'
wage, can also lead to a "prisoner's dilemma" type of
inflationary process without any obvious excess demand. (See
Lal 1977).

Thus, say the price of imported food rises and is expected
to continue to rise, and hence workers' current and future cost
of living rises. Workers concerned, for the above reasons,
with real wage differentials and who are bargaining with their
employers for the next year's wage will have to take a view as
to whether or not the other workers who form their reference
groups, will try and offset the increase in the past cost of
living, as well as any expected increases in the future cost of
living. For the latter, they have to form expectations about
the likely extent of the rise in prices expected in the future
by other workers. Thus in order to prevent the erosion of their
differentials they are all likely to negotiate money wage rises
which correspond to the highest expected future price increase,
even if they would all be willing to accept a real wage cut if
the differentials could be maintained).

Finally, if for the above reasons, money wages are sticky
in these labour markets, any relative wage change which may be
required on resource allocation grounds, in the face of long

run changes in the demand and supply of different types of labour, can only come about through a rise in money wages in the sectors experiencing a medium run shortage of labour. For these reasons, modern industrial labour markets are likely to have an inherent inflationary bias, which of course can always be exacerbated by incautious and unwarranted demand expansion.

POLICY DILEMMAS

Increased Unemployment and Inflation - Can the Rising "Discomfort Index" Be Tamed by Deflation?

In the previous section we may have partially succeeded in rescuing the major Keynesian insights concerning the labour market from the rational expectations onslaught. These are the stickiness of industrial money wages, as well as the paradox that workers may be willing to accept a cut in real wages through a rise in the general price level, but not through cuts in their money wages. These insights were obviously of great practical significance in the depression years when the General Theory was formulated, and its central message, that aggregate demand should be expanded, valid. Does it still have policy relevance in the current problems of stagflation in OECD countries?

Keynes explicitly recognised (see Keynes 1936) that the aggregate supply schedule would most likely have the shape in Fig. II. That is before his full employment barrier could be reached money wages and prices would start to rise. It is in this nether region that the OECD world has lived for most of the post World War II period.

Since the early 1970's, as is now recognised even by monetarists (see Friedman's Nobel lecture), the two massive OPEC oil price rises of 1973-1974, and 1978-80 have shifted this aggregate supply curve upwards. Governments have then faced the unenviable choice of either maintaining existing levels of employment but accomodating the oil price rise through a rise in the general price level (or its rate of change) or else by reducing employment in order to maintain the old price level (or its rate of change). They have usually chosen some unemployment along with some inflation. The observed movement from X to X^1, then gives the impression that they have moved along a positively sloped Phillips curve. But this is an optical illusion, for it is composed of a shift in the aggregate supply curve and the normal Phillips type short-run cyclical movements along the new curve.

Some statistical confirmation of this process which would yield the stagflationary trends witnessed in most OECD countries in the 1970's is provided in a model of wage inflation estimated for the USA by Perry. This distinguishes between a norm rate of wage increase, and the usual cyclical Phillips curve. Perry shows that this model works pretty well in explaining wage inflation trends in the USA in the 1960's and 1970's. The 'norm' around which the Phillips relationship works has shifted up substantially during the 1970's as compared with the 1960's. This shift in the 'norm' of wage increase is not entirely due to the oil price rise but according to Perry was initiated by the effects of higher inflationary expectations engendered by the excess demand created to finance the Vietnam war. Perry then simulates the response of wage inflation to a deep recession, using his estimated wage equation. He begins his simulations with the actual values, in the first quarter of 1980, of the unemployment rate (5.7%) and wage inflation rate (9.2%), and considers alternative policies of a sustained recession, and one in which over 5 years there is both a recession and recovery. He estimates the rate of wage inflation on two alternative assumptions (a) that there is no change in the wage norm, (b) that it shifts down "by one half the change in the rate of wage inflation after two years, by three-fourths of the change in the rate after 3 years, and by the full change in the rate after four years" (Perry, p. 25). With a sustained recession in which the unemployment rate is maintained at 9% for 5 years, the rate of wage inflation is reduced to 8% in without the norm shift, and 4.6% with the norm shift. If instead there is a recession in which the unemployment rate rises to 8.6% in two years, and thereafter falls, so that it is 5.9% after the same five years, the rate of wage inflation falls to 8.1%, and then rises back again to 9.2% without a norm shift, and falls to 7.1% with a norm shift after 5 years.

Apart from illustrating the cruel policy dilemmas posed, these simulations also show that it is unlikely that inflation (at least in the USA) can be lowered (on the best assumptions) by more than about 4 percentage points, even with the continuance of an unemployment rate which is twice the current one. One really must believe that the costs of an extra four percent of inflation are tremendous if one is to be sanguine about the real output and unemployment losses associated with an unemployment rate of 9% for the USA. I remain unconvinced by the various horror stories about hyper-inflation which have convinced many governments to wage a war on inflation, for the reasons set out in Lal (1977). Moreover, many of the social costs (chiefly distributional) arising from unanticipated inflation can be offset by promoting general indexation to the GDP deflator.

The latter form of indexation does not 'lock in' the economy in the face of 'real' shocks, as would happen if the index chosen was the consumer price index – and which is the index assumed in most discussions of indexation. It might also mitigate some of the money wage push based on the "prisoner's dilemma" type argument sketched in the last part. For it could moderate the inflationary expectations in 'atomistic' money wage bargaining, as long as the expected rate of inflation is higher than the realised rate (as seems all too likely when the highest expected rate of inflation becomes the wage norm of workers concerned with relativities).

'Supply Side' Economics – Does Keynesian Fiscalism need Revision?

Additionally, various policies to improve the 'supply' side of the economy through raising overall productivity and increasing the flexibility of the economy to adjust to shocks, could also ease the stagflationary pressures of the 1980's. The most important of these are a commitment to maintain open economies, help rather than hinder the accompanying adjustment in traded goods industries by eschewing subsidies to declining industries, and above all in ensuring that energy price rises are speedily passed on to consumers. The various restrictions on ecological grounds to the development or exploitation of alternative energy sources also need to be eased. Restrictions imposed by subsidised housing policies which restrict labour mobility could be lifted.

Many of these measures of so-called 'supply side' economics, concern the reversal of various inefficient microeconomic interventions that have mushroomed in the post World War II world in most OECD countries, as a result of the increasing politicisation of economic policy to serve the often mutually conflicting interests of diverse sectional groups in these democracies. In part this has been the result of the rise and victory of Keynesian fiscalism, and part of the intuitive appeal of many monetarist panaceas – constant money supply rules, and constitutional provisions for ensuring balance budgets – lies in the growing public perception that the costs of many government interventions (in terms of efficiency) have been greater than their avowed benefits (in terms of equity or stability).

It is thus in the area of fiscal policy, its links with monetary policy, and the possibility of delinking the macro-stabilisation as opposed to the micro-economic functions of the government budget that in my view the major revision of the Keynesian policy perspective is required. To pinpoint these revisions it is useful to show why, though there may be a grain of good sense in the monetarist desire to put governments in the strait jacket of fixed money supply growth targets, their policy prescriptions are not likely to be feasible.

Constant Money Supply Growth Rules

I do not in this paper wish to argue against the monetarist desire to see governments follow a constant money growth rate rule (CMGR). Its desirability has been questioned on the fundamental ground that, in theory, even in a monetarist world of rational expectations money is not neutral (see Hahn 1980, Buiter 1980, Tobin and Buiter in Stein). I am more concerned with the feasibility of modern OECD governments actually following CMGR. The ensuing discussion will also hopefully show, why Keynesians are often baffled by monetarist assertions that they have found new 'truths' from what are essentially analytically the same monetary model.

The existing policy differences between so-called "monetarists" and Keynesians reflect in part the long-standing controversy between the banking and currency schools on the nature of "money". The differences can be put most simply (as Wicksell did) in terms of two alternative types of monetary structure. The first is one in which there is only metallic money, or else a hundred percent reserve requirement for banks, or else a fixed and unchangeable reserve requirement for banks linking their credit in a fixed proportion to some 'hard money' base. In this type of monetary system it is not difficult to show that the classical quantity theory will hold (see Wicksell, Hawtrey, Hicks) and also that direct control of the exogenous monetary base will be feasible.

The second type of monetary system is a pure credit system which has no metallic money (or fixed link to a metallic reserve base). The promissory paper IOU's of the various traders and the banks which form the Banking System, are the 'bank notes' or currency of this system (see Hawtrey Ch. 1, and Hicks 1977 Ch. III, for a clear account of the workings of a pure credit economy). In such an economy, it can also be shown that quantity theory type results will no longer hold. For suppose, following Hawtrey, we have a pure credit economy in which the IOU's of market participants are the medium of exchange. Bankers are dealers in debt. Moreover these debts can be expressed in an accounting unit. "The debts of the whole community can be settled by transfers in the banker's books or by the delivery of documents, such as bank notes, representative of the banker's obligations". (Hawtrey, p. 4). The possible instability of the resulting credit economy is graphically described by Hawtrey as follows (p. 13):

"Suppose some of the merchants, in the hope of extending their business, give increased orders to the manufacturers. The manufacturers will forthwith borrow more than usual from their bankers. They wll urge on the business of manufacture, will pay more to their employees, and will receive greater profits in proportion to their greater output. They and their employees will have more to spend; the retailers will dispose of more goods, and will take over more from the merchants; the merchants will give yet further orders to the manufacturers. The manufacturers, finding their productive capacity overstrained, will quote higher prices to the merchants; the merchants, being unable to supply the retailers fast enough or to maintain their stocks of goods, will raise prices to the retailers, and the retailers will raise prices to the public. The general rise of prices will involve a proportional increase of borrowing to finance a given output of goods, over and above the increase necessitated by the increase of output. This increase of borrowing, meaning an increase in the volume of bank credit, will further stimulate activity. "This process is what is commonly called an inflation of credit. Where will it end? An indefinite expansion seems to be in the immediate interest of merchants and bankers alike. The continuous and progressive rise of prices makes it profitable to hold goods in stock, and the rate of interest which the merchant who holds such goods is prepared to pay is correspondingly high. Thus the merchant and the banker share between them a larger rate of profit on a larger turn-over. The credit created for the purposes of production becomes purchasing power in the hands of the people engaged in production; the greater the amount of credit created, the greater will be the amount of purchasing power and the better the market for the sale of all kinds of goods. The better the market the greater the demand for credit".

It might be thought that this instability can be prevented by the distributional 'wealth' effects which a general movement

in prices by transferring purchasing power from debtors to
creditors, entails. But this, as Hicks (1977) emphasises,
ignores the effects of such price movements on psychology. "As
soon as prices move sufficiently for people to extrapolate -to
base their expectations of future prices not upon current
prices but upon the way prices have been changing - a
destabilising force is set up which is bound to swamp the much
weaker stabilising power of the 'wealth effect'. That is the
basic cause of the instability". (Hicks 1977, p. 120).

Furthermore, in this pure credit economy, it is obvious
that the stock of credit (which would be equivalent to the
"money supply" in the pure metallic or rigid metallic exchange
standard) is purely endogenous.

It has been recognized by all sides in the controversy
over money that the key issue is the endogenity or exogeneity
of the money supply. Thus, in his reply to Kaldor's (in our
view devastating) critique of what Kaldor calls Friedmanism,
Friedman states "Professor Kaldor makes one central point: that
changes in the money supply must be regarded as the result, not
the cause of changes in economic activity... Establish this
point, and his case against the monetarists is firm; pins move
with the cycle; money moves with the cycle; this is evidence
of neither a pin theory of the cycle nor a monetary theory of
the cycle but of the pervasive influence of cyclical
fluctuations" (Friedman 1970a p. 23) Quite!

But, if the logical possibility of a pure credit economy
with its obvious endogenity of the money supply is conceded,
surely it must be a question of institutional fact, whether or
not a particular economy's monetary institutions are better
described as being closer to the "hard money" (whether in terms
of a pure metallic or metallic exchange or fixed immutable rule
reserve based) system or to that of a pure credit economy.
Moreover, human institutions themselves are not immutable so
that over time "money" may evolve from a "hard" to pure credit
money. This is likely, given the inexorable drive of profit
maximising economic agents to substitute cheaper means of
payment. Thus, historical evidence based say on the operations
of a 'hard money' system will be inappropriate if the current
and future system is going to be one of the pure credit sort.

The most casual empiricism will show that the industrial
economies have moved closer and closer towards becoming pure
credit economies. The consequent difficulty of describing such
a system in "hard money" terms is vividly shown by the great
difficulties increasingly encountered in defining some
exogenous monetary base which as in a 'hard money' system can
be taken to determine the quantity of 'money' in the economy.
"The creation of a 'substitute hard money' by control over the

quantity of some sort (or sorts) of money is continually defeated by human ingenuity in the invention of other sorts... Hawtrey and Keynes were surely right in holding that they were dealing with a system that had no automatic stabiliser; a system which needed to be stabilised by policy" (Hicks, ibid, p. 120).

However, the monetarists maybe forgiven for reading into the Keynesian theory of liquidity preference an implicit hard money, 'reserve based' type monetary system, in which the money supply is exogenous. But for Keynesians the liquidity trap, and the presumed inelasticity of investment, make monetary policy – either through changes in the money stock or interest rates – an ineffective instrument to alter aggregate demand. The route is then left open for fiscal policy, as the major macroeconomic policy instrument.

The Instrument of Monetary Control – Was Hawtrey Right After All?

The Keynesian revisionist Hicks has questioned the assumption of the interest inelasticity of investment, by resurrecting the debate between Hawtrey and Keynes. For Keynes it was the long run rate of interest which affected investment. He rejected Hawtrey's doctrine that it was the short term rate of interest on bank lending, summarised by the Bank Rate in the UK (to which such short term rates were tied) which "had a direct effect on the activity of trade and industry" (Hicks 1977, p. 120). Keynes concerned as he was with the propensity to invest in fixed capital rather than changes in the willingness of traders to hold stocks, as a primary cause of economic fluctuations, was not much impressed by Hawtrey's arguments. But as Hicks rightly notes, "it does not follow... that a direct operation upon the decision whether or not to undertake fixed capital investment (the kind of effect which Keynes – at least in his first phase – thought to be capable of being exercised through the long rate of interest) is a convenient or even, a practicable way of exercising control. There are few expansion plans, even though they are to be mainly financed from retained profits, or from long term capital raised upon the market, which do not depend upon the availability of bank credit at some stage of the process. The availability of bank credit can still affect timing. it is the sense of the importance of timing which is expressed, in Hawtrey's model, by his emphasis on the short-term rate of interst". (Hicks 1977, p. 126).

If, through the Bank Rate mechanism, the Central Bank can

affect expectations about the likely course of future short
term rates of interest, and thereby the availability of credit
in the economy, a less blunt and unwieldy stabilisation
instrument is available than that of changing the size and
composition of the government budget. This instrument may be
particularly effective, if the OECD world is moving towards a
pure credit type international monetary system, with flexible
exchange rates. Then, each national monetary authority is
nothing more than a member bank in the pure credit
international banking system. With capital mobile, it might be
thought member banks would not be able to effect their national
short term rate of interest in such a system. If exchange rates
are flexible, and market participants (who are international)
have some expectations about the 'normal' level of a country's
exchange rate, this need not happen. For, if the country's
Central Bank were to raise short term interest rates, to stem a
boom say (or to engineer a slump), the exchange rate would rise
above its 'normal' level, thus restoring international
interest-rate parity and also choking off any capital inflows
(as the exchange rate would be expected in time to depreciate
to its 'normal' level — a process which would also be aided by
the trade balance effects of the exchange rate appreciation).
The high domestic short term interest rate and exchange rate
would have the requisite depressive effects on aggregate demand
but also on its composition as the high exchange rate would
penalise the traded goods sector as seems to be happening
currently in the UK. Conversely in order to engineer a boom
the reverse set of policies could be followed.

In this process in a pure credit economy, the money supply
can not be directly effected and need not even be a policy
target. Though, of course, indirectly the restrictive credit
policy (if it works) will affect the total supply of bank
money. But this also means that, though the Central Bank can be
given directional instructions about the movement in interest
rates in the light of particular conjunctures, precise
mechanical rules cannot be provided. The "feel" of the market
emphasised by 19th century writers on money (such as Thornton)
is of importance because it emphasises that the important point
is how the existing market sentiments, based on changing
judgements about an irreducible uncertain future, can be
changed.

Since Ricardo, however, there have been those who have
wished to control credit money by sme device which would make
it behave like metallic money. The modern day monetarists are
merely following in their footsteps. But, if our argument is
right, any mechanical rule based monetary policy (in a pure

credit economy) is a will o' the wisp, and this applies equally to the CMGR.

If, however, Hawtrey's Bank Rate or some such policy instrument could be devised to manage national credit economies in a world wide credit system, with flexible exchange rates between different national 'monies', then the conflicting pressures currently exercised on the government budget could be eased.

The Budget and Promotion of Social Efficiency – The End of Fiscalism?

The government budget essentially deals with the 'real' side of the economy, namely equity (through transfer payments) and allocative efficiency (through taxes and subsidies). The micro-economic public interventions which are justified in order to correct or adjust (in a second best way) to the distortions that make laissez-faire outcomes socially sub-optimal in any real world economy, are to a large extent reflected in the structure of taxes and subsidies and the provision of public goods through the government budget. The criteria for judging the desirability of such interventions, their form and size, should be based on the principles of welfare economics. One of the more serious muddles associated with the identification of Keynesiansism with fiscalism is the mixing up of these esentially welfare economic considerations with those of monetary stabilisation. As such, instead of assessing the relative social costs and benefits of different types of public expenditure, these have often been judged primarily by their effects on short run conjunctural problems. The "supply side" inefficiencies that have increasingly hardened the economic arteries of OECD countries are partly due to the relative neglect of social efficiency considerations in the design of fiscal policies.

This does not mean that the government's actions in terms of its budget, and more particularly its borrowing, will not have monetary effects. What it does mean is that, in the design of budgetary policy, the desirability of borrowing should be judged by the social rates of return to the uses made of such borrowing and not by its effects on the "money" supply or aggregate demand. The latter effects should be the concern of the Central Bank. But if it is to act as a true bank in a pure credit economy, it must not be the government's creature, extending unlimited credit to its masters at less than market rates. The government's credit rating will undoubtedly be better than many other market participants because, if nothing else, of its exclusive power to exact tribute from its subjects in the form of taxation. If it is thought necessary to affect credit in the economy, the instrument chosen (say influencing the structure of short term rates of interest) should also affect the cost of borrowing by the government and its agents in the wider public sector.

Does International Credit Need To Be Stabilised?

What of the international economy? Will not a pure credit international monetary system also be inherently unstable and what is the monetary instrument that could be used to stabilise it and who will wield the instrument? It would seem that a world central bank is called for. But this is infeasible given the existing reluctance of nation-states to relinquish what they consider to be an essential element of their soveriegnty, the right to influence the levels of activity within their economies. (see Lal 1980).

In a world of floating exchange rates, each national monetary authority should be able to affect the levels of economic activity during the cycle, even though no mechanical rules can be prescribed for their policy actions. Similarly, through the well-established lender of last resort functions of a Central Bank, the adverse effects of banking panics which maybe expected to strike any pure credit economy, particularly at the top of an unsustainable boom can be mitigated.

But with the vast growth of international banking, and the large OPEC oil surpluses which it is called upon to recycle, is there not a similar danger of a banking panic on the international scale? The danger most often cited by many faint hearted observers of international capital markets is the simultaneous default by a number of economically shaky developing countries of their increasingly large loans from the international commercial banks. Might not such a default trigger an international banking panic? If it does, where is the lender of last resort on the international scene? (see Kindleberger for a detailed account of past national banking panics, and fears about future international ones).

The major feature of banking panics and the consequent disastrous destruction of credit, liquidity, output and employment, they lead to is that, in such a crisis, loans to perfectly creditworthy borrowers are also called in at the same time as from those whose future prospects are more shaky. To stem the panic it is necessary to assure the financial markets that credit will still continue to be extended to those whose 'real' future prospects remain good. The rule which Bagheot laid down for a lender of last resort was "that loans should be granted to all on the basis of sound collateral" (Kindleberger,

p. 175). But this makes the terms as well as the bills which the Central Bank is willing to discount, to halt the run out of real and illiquid financial assets into money, a matter of judgement. Who will perform this rediscounting, and form the necessary qualitative judgements in the face of an international banking panic?

The answer to the first question is that, the rediscounting must ultimately be done by the member Central Banks of the international banking system in whose national jurisdictions the international banks are domiciled. Moreover, if it is largely the fear of developing countries defaulting which sets off the panic, the so-called conditional lending of the IMF provides an adequate mechanism for exercising the judgement about the future prospects of the 'borrowers', enforcing measures which improve those prospects, and arranging for a rescheduling of their debts which prevents the liquidify of the international system from being eroded. Thus in effect there already exist in the world-wide credit economy, means for preventing an international banking panic. But as an essential element of this mechanism is the "conditionality" of IMF borrowing by a country, which then unclogs the international credit mechanism, it is vital that this 'surveillance' function of the IMF not be eroded by the extant political pressures by Third World countries to abolish such conditionality.

Conclusions

We have by now covered a lot of ground. As is obvious, the problems we have dealt with can be illumined by many Keynesian insights, but not surprisingly some (particularly these concerning the use of the budget as a stabiliser) need to be amended. The policy debate raked up by the monetarists is in many ways a phony debate, but of course money matters. But "money" itself is not an immutable 'thing'. It is an institutional artifact whose nature changes with economic evolution. The current day monetarists hanker after a credit system that can be made to work like a "hard money" system by some mechanical device. This we have argued is not feasible, unless the efficiency losses which would be associated with a return to a "hard money" system are accepted, and such a monetary system is in fact established. When, as in the current movement towards a pure credit system (in both the domestic and international spheres), money is endogenous, it is illusory to hope to directly control some "exogenous" monetary aggregate. The use of the short run interest rate instrument avowed by Hawtrey but eschewed by both Keynesians and monetarists alike, perhaps needs to be revived. But even if some such effective instrument for <u>indirectly</u> controlling credit "money" can be found, it is unlikely, that the war on inflation can be won through politically acceptable deflations. Whilst for those who correctly argue that some (large enough) dose of deflation would halt inflation in its tracks, one can only ask:, but what is gained? at what cost? and once economic recovery takes place, why should the inflationary bias of industrial labour markets disappear? The gravest disservice the monetarists may have done is to have fuelled a belief that there are simple answers to the current stagflationary conjuncture, which if adopted will not require any of the above questions to be answered.

As any acute reader of this paper will be aware, in this third part, I have been merely putting together or refurbishing many of the insights of Sir John Hicks. If I have had little to say about the so-called Post-Keynesians who live by the Cam, this is only in part because of my upbringing! It is rather because their recent policy views, as expressed for instance by the collective noun "New Cambridge", are in my view illogical, and I have attempted to substantiate this elsewhere (Lal 1979a).

If the essential long term cure for the West's current problems is to remove the plaque from its economic arteries, a protectionist policy of turning inwards and substituting a market by a command economy can only spell disaster. Though it may be best to learn to live with unavoidable 'cost-push' type inflation, in the long run the answer must lie in easing the current conjunctural straitjacket, by working on policies to improve the supply side of the economy. The most basic revision of Keynesian doctrine required may be to bring back an appreciation of the continuing importance of productivity, profitability and thrift - factors which for too long seemed to have been denigrated by Keynesian modes of analysis. Demand management, Keynesian or monetarist, may be less important than replenishing the springs of enterprise which have been the ultimate mainsprings of the secular boom we have enjoyed since the Second World War.

113

FIGURE I.

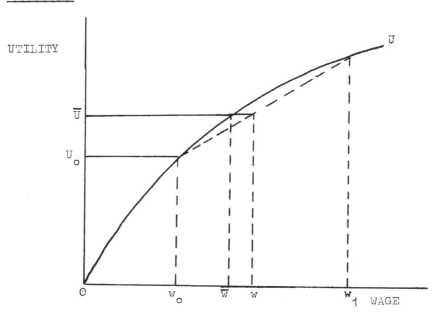

FIGURE II.

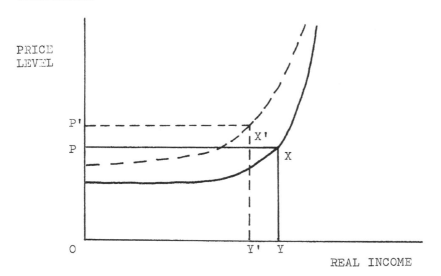

1)   Thus assume that there are n workers in the firm's labour pool. There is a probability p, that during the relevant period (say a year) only n_o (n_o n_1) of these workers can profitably be employed. Hours per worker are assumed fixed. The value marginal product of n_o workers employed in the two states of nature are V_o, (when employment is n_o) and V_1) when it is n_1). During the periode when $n_1{}^o$-n_o) workers are unemployed, the workers are laid off at random. Then consider two alternative labour contracts from the viewpoint of both employers and workers.

(I)   Fluctuating Wage and Employment

    The employed workers are paid a fluctuating wage equal to their value marginal product in the two states of nature, whilst unemployed workers receive nothing. Firms are risk neutral; workers are risk averse. The profit maximizing expected wage bill of the firm E(W) is then given by :

$$p. \; V_o \; n_o + (1-p) \; V_1 \cdot n_1 = E(W) \underline{\hspace{2cm}} \text{(E1)}$$

As the probability of any worker being laid off and receiving no income if state of nature n_o prevails is $p \; [1-n_1/n_o]$ his utility over the year with a fluctuating wage and employment level, U(V) is :

$$U(V) = p \; \left[(1-n_o/n_1) \; U(0) = (n_o/n_1) \; U(V_o) \right] + (1-p) \; U(V_1)$$

or

$$U(V) = p \cdot (n_o/n_1) \; U(V_o) + (1-p) \; U(V_1) \underline{\hspace{1.5cm}} (L_1)$$

(assuming U(0) = 0.).

(II) Fixed Wage and Fluctuating Employment. Suppose next that, instead employers offer a fixed wage but fluctuating employment contract, at a fixed wage rate W less than the expected wage in (I), namely

$\overline{w}$ <pV_o + (1-p) V_1, so that their expected wage bill E($\overline{W}$)
is given by

$$(p \cdot n_o + (1-p)n_1) \; \overline{w} = E(\overline{W}) \underline{\hspace{2cm}} \text{(E2)}$$

As $E(\overline{W}) < E(W)$, employers stand to gain from offering such a contract.

The workers utility is now given by

$$U(\overline{W}) = U(\overline{w}) \left[p \frac{n_0}{n_1} + (1-p) \right] \underline{\hspace{3cm}} (L2)$$

As $U'(y) > 0$; $U''(y) < 0$, $U(\overline{w}) - U(v_0) \geq U(v_1) - U(\overline{w})$, and hence from (L1) and (L2) there will be some $\overline{w}$, for which $U(\overline{W}) \geq U(V)$, and workers too will prefer a fixed wage (less than the expected wage) and fluctuating employment contract.

2) We now consider an alternative contract –

III <u>Fixed Wage Employment</u> – Employers now offer a fixed wage $w^* < \overline{w}$ and full employment. They will be indifferent or better off than under contract II, as long as the expected wage bill.

$$E(W^*) = w^* \, n_1 \leqslant \left[pn_0 + (1-p) \, n_1 \right] \overline{w} = E(\overline{W}) \underline{\hspace{1.5cm}} (E3)$$

Workers will prefer this third type of contract as long as

$$U(w^*) \geqslant U(\overline{w}) \left[p \frac{n_0}{n_1} + (1-p) \right] \underline{\hspace{3cm}} (L3)$$

As the term in square brackets is less than one, they will prefer the contract offered with $w^* < \overline{w}$.

References

G.A. Akerlof and M. Miyazaki (1980): "The Implicit Contract Theory of Unemployment meets the Wage Bill Argument", Review of Economic Studies, January 1980.

C. Azariadis (1975): "Implicit Contracts and Underemployment Equilibria", Journal of Political Economy, December 1975.

C. Azariadis (1976): "On the Incidence of Unemployment", Review of Economic Studies, February 1976.

M.N Baily (1976): "Contract Theory and the Moderation of Inflation by Recession and by Controls", Brookings Papers in Economic Activity, 3, 1976.

R.J. Barro (1976): "Rational Expectations and the Role of Monetary Policy", Journal of Monetary Economics, No. 2, 1976.

R.J. Barro (1977): "Long-Term Contracting Sticky Prices and Monetary Policy", Journal of Monetary Economics, No, 2, 1977.

K. Brunner and A. Meltzer (1977): Stabilisation of the Domestic and International Economy (Carnegie-Rochester Conference Series, Vol. 5, North Holland, 1977).

M. Friedman (1968): "The Role of Monetary Policy", American Economic Review, March 1968 reprinted in M. Friedman (1969).

M. Friedman (1970a): "Reply by Milton Friedman and A. Rejonder, Lloyds Bank Review, October 1970.

M. Friedman (1977): "Nobel Lecture: Inflation and Unemployment", Journal of Political Economy, June 1977.

R.J. Gordon (1976): "Recent Developments in the Theory of Inflation and Unemployment", Journal of Monetary Economics, 1976, reprinted in Lundberg (ed.) (1976), op.cit.

R.G. Hawrey (1950): Currency and Credit, 4th edition, (Longmans, 1950).

J.R. Hicks (1965): Capital and Growth, (Oxford, 1965).

J.R. Hicks (1967): Critical Essays in Monetary Theory, (Oxford, 1967).
    - (1974): The Crisis in Keynesian Economics (Blackwells, 1974). - (1977): Economic Perspectives - Further Essay on Money and Growth (Oxford, 1977).
    - (1979): Causality in Economics (Blackwells, 1979).

N. Kaldor (1970): "The New Monetarism", Lloyds Bank Review, July 1970.

J.M. Keynes (1936): The General Theory of Employment Interest and Money (Macmillan, 1936).
    - (1937): "The General Theory of Employment", Quarterly Journal of Economics, February 1937, reprinted in J.M. Keynes Collected Works XIV, op.cit.

C.P. Kindleberger (1978): <u>Manias, Panics and Crashes</u> (Basic Books, New York, 1978).

D. Lal (1977): <u>Unemployment and Wage Inflation in Industrial Economies</u> (OECD, Paris, 1977).

D. Lal (1978): <u>Poverty, Power and Prejudice - The North-South Confrontation</u> (Fabian Research Series, 340, Fabian Society, London, December 1978).

D. Lal (1979): "Theories of Industrial Wage Structures: A Review", <u>Indian Journal of Industrial Relations</u>, November 1979, reprinted in <u>World Bank Reprint Series</u>.

D. Lal (1979a): "Comment on Managed Trade Between Industrial Countries" in R. Major (ed.): <u>Britains Trade and Exchange Rate Policy</u>, (NIESR Heinemann 1979).

D. Lal (1980): <u>A Liberal International Economic Order, The International Monetary System and Economic Development</u>, Princeton Essays in International Finance, No. 139, (Princeton N.J., 1980).

R.E. Lucas Jr. (1972): "Expectations and the Neutrality of Money", <u>Journal of Economic Theory</u>, April 1972.

R.E. Lucas (1977): "Understanding Business Cycles", in Brunner and Meltzer (eds) (1977).

J.F. Muth (1961): "Rational Expectations and the Theory of Price Movements", <u>Econometrica</u>? June 1961.

W.Y. Oi (1962): "Labour as a Quasi-Fixed Factor", <u>Journal of Political Economy</u>, December 1962.

G.L. Perry (1980): "Inflation in Theory and Practice", <u>Brookings Papers on Economic Activity</u>, 1: 1980.

T.J. Sargent and N. Wallace (1975): "'Rational' Expectations, The Optimal Monetary Instrument, and the Optimal Money Supply Rule", <u>Journal of Political Economy</u>, April 1975.

K. Wicksell: <u>Interest and Prices</u>.

COMMENTS ON LAL'S PAPER

Roger Tarling, Department of Applied Economics, Cambridge University

I would like to begin by referring to an exchange between Deepak Lal and Robert Neild at a conference on Britain's trade and exchange-rate policy in June 1979 organised by the National Institute of Economic and Social Research in London (see Major). Lal stated there that a number of papers 'show clearly that modern trade theory is concerned in particular with providing rigorous rankings of alternative policies (including protection) when one or other of the perfectly competitive assumptions (including full employment) breaks down'. From that position, he argued the case that for the U.K. 'the proper policy is not protection but various combinations of domestic taxes and subsidies'. I do not intend to deal with protectionism but, as a member of the Cambridge Economic Policy Group, I wish to establish some reasons for different policy prescriptions and explain how I see these as originating in and affecting the labour market.

The crux of the debate to which I have referred is not a question of the interpretation of international trade theory but the difference in views on the nature of competition. Conventional trade theory is however an excellent arena in which to discuss the question. Competition, in this context, is about response to price and cost differences. Any factor or process which interferes with the mechanism by which these differences are accommodated to achieve equilibrium must be a distortion, or imperfection, which should either be removed or countered. Optimal solutions will not be attained but we can seek to attain second best solutions.

In his paper for this conference, Lal has produced as excellent critique of current thinking. In these hard times, we may unite in opposition to monetarism but not perhaps in our view of alternative policy packages. To recognise firm-specific training (making labour a quasi-fixed factor of production) and using irreducible uncertainty to explain disequilibrium against a paradigm described by neoclassical economics is not an obstacle to recognising the extent to which strict adherence to monetarist policies closes down the options of industrial sectors and leads to the collapse of domestic activity: the macro-economic consequences are agreed. But, unless we recognise the extent of our differences in the view of competition, we will continue to disagree on whether outcomes are 'second best' and what supply side policies are worthy of consideration.

Oligopoly in the product market, real wage rigidity and labour markets in which relatively homogeneous labour are faced with heterogeneous opportunities characterise the real world. But oligopolistic competition sits uneasily in a neoclassical framework. Ultimately the validity of any economic theory rests on how well it represents reality. Thus, if neoclassical theory is to have any relevance, the basic mechanisms of the real economy must operate as that theory postulates. Only then can the real world phenomena be safely relegated to footnotes or accommodated in partial models. The nature of oligopoly, and of its associated institutions, is however constantly changing and its dynamism is an outcome of a complex interaction of economic, political and social forces. Neoclassical economics provide a window with a very limited view of the process. And so, Lal condemns Keynesian fiscalism in the post war period. But, just as Lal himself denounces deflation as an anti-inflationary policy because of its cost, so too may one question the social cost of adopting his 'supply side' revisions.

Let us consider deflation on the scale apparently required to reduce inflation or otherwise alleviate a balance of payments constraint. Its principal danger is that it can destroy the internationally competitive sectors of production. We have seen what import penetration can do: a very clear example is what has happened in the cutlery trades in the U.K. where it is the mass production sector, that part of the industry where technical progress is most rapid, which is being destroyed by low cost foreign competition, leaving a residual activity based on specialist products and low technology processes (Craig, Rubery, Tarling and Wilkinson 1980). This, of course, is not a certain outcome; a counter-example is provided by the jute industry where a strong employers association has helped to accommodate transition in the face of low cost foreign competition and technical changes involved in the use of polypropylene to manufacture product substitutes (Craig, Rubery, Tarling and Wilkinson 1979).

The purpose of a macro-economic protectionist policy is to avoid unnecessarily high levels of unemployment; at the same time, the maintenance of domestic demand provides markets for domestic production which in turn provides the basis for economic development. In a neoclassical world, this would be inefficient but, if the response to competition is the collapse of industries and of demand, the 'market solution' is a very dangerous policy to pursue. Of course, the weakest go to the wall first – but what if they are all weak, what then remains? Supply side policies would need to be remarkably effective to preserve the manufacturing base.

Protection may take the form of devaluation or direct intervention in trade flows. It has been argued that protection by tariffs may require large and increasing tariffs; however, it is also the case that devaluation would probably have to be large and continuous. It has been argued that protection by quota or tariff will induce retaliation and be self-defeating (we have given an answer to that in CEPG 1980, pp. 16-18). But is is also necessary to consider what would happen in the case of devaluation when recession and deflation give a zero balance of payments - why then should exchange rates move in the right direction to achieve full employment?

Comparison of the phases of transition suggests that protection provides better terms of trade and does not cut real incomes in the short term, whereas a devaluation strategy requires that initially prices rise relative to money wages and that the cut in real wages persists. But, to achieve this, the policy package must include a succesful incomes policy to prevent the unhappy situation of accelerated inflation without the restoration of full employment.

Lal (1979) has stated 'if the real-wage rigidity is the only distortion, the optimal policy would be a general wage subsidy (financed through lump-sum taxation) equating the actual rigid real wage to the lower shadow wage (which in this case would be the notional perfectly competitive wage)'. As Chart 1, I have appended to this note a chart printed in CEPG (1980) showing the path of real post-tax wage settlements in the U.K. in the post-war period. It shows, to simplify, that incomes policies have worked - for a short while, after which there is a recovery to 'trend'. In my view, which includes oligopolistic competition, this is not a measure of distortionary tendency, resisting the claim of profits: real wages are no longer to be determined as a residual.[1]

There is, however, an useful point of discussion over whether the 'trend' is anything more than a statistical artifact. A study of the evolution of collective bargaining in the U.K. which I have undertaken with Wilkinson[2] has shown that national collective bargaining evolved by the 1920's and that the institutional framework has been evolving ever since. The conflict in the determination of ex ante real wages (at settlement) arises partly because an employer's interest lies in profitability and the price of one product whereas his employees are concerned with wages in relation to the whole basket of consumption goods. In a closed economy, with prices a mark-up on costs, we must have a theory of the distribution of income between wages and profits; in an open economy, the theory must incorporate the role of the terms of trade between manufactured goods and primary products as well as productivity. Thus the correct expression of the 'trend' in ex post real wages is as a function of real per capita national income. The evolutionary surges in the institutional framework for bargaining can be shown to be related to the variations in real per capita national income and used to explain how real wage settlements are returned to their 'trend'. This trend, however, is in the long run jointly determined with the bargaining framework and is dependent on the processes of social and economic development.

Lal (1979, p. 35) has also suggested that 'the presumed real-wage rigidity ... is probably peculiar to this country (the U.K.)'. However, recent work by John Eatwell and Joop Odink suggest that Dutch real disposable income per hour bears an uncommon resemblance to Chart 1, in particular the behaviour of wages during and immediately after the Tinbergen incomes policy of the late 1950's.

Whatever policies are adopted to resolve the problems of industrial countries, none can hope to eliminate in the short term the high levels of unemployment. But is is argued by some (for example, Lal 1977) and in his present paper that the types of employment policy currently in use, for example training and job support schemes through wage subsidy, are methods for equating actual wages with the shadow wage. If, however, the root cause of the problem lies in oligopolistic competition which is not amenable to massage to bring it into line with a 'better second best' solution, then these policies may be little more than an exercise in 'window-dressing' if they reduce administrative levels of unemployment and may achieve in practice only a reshuffling of the burden of unemployment among different individuals.

In Keynesian macro-economic models, unemployment is the residual between (potential) labour supply and the level of employment determined by output. The theoretical basis of the relationship between employment and output was derived by Brechling (1965) and extensively developed by Ball and St. Cyr (1966). In essence, it is a short period cost-minimising solution in a neoclassical framework with a U-shaped curve for wage cost per hour based on the relationship between paid and productive hours. But, if we reject the competitive assumptions of the framework, we must reassess the usefulness of such a relationship. Empirically, there is evidence that the specification of the relationship for various countries has given rise to highly unstable parameter estimates. Unless we are committed to the theoretical framework, we should consider replacing that relationship with a more appropriate one, rather than massaging the specification or the residuals.

In an alternative framework on which I am working (Tarling, 1980) employers are assumed in the short-run to maximise competitive advantage by minimising average unit labour costs. Employers adopt strategies in the product and labour markets to achieve this. In stable product markets, they seek to gain market control and control over the organisation of production and then create internal labour markets by which they internalise labour cost adjustments as much as possible. Peak demands may be subcontracted to other suppliers and the burden of recessions can be passed on by reducing and shortening order books of supplies. Labour, if available, can be employed on a subcontracted basis, such as outwork and homework. Other firms survive by adopting low technology processes and having flexible unit labour costs by employing weakly organised groups of labour at low cost with poor terms and conditions of employment: high wastage rates combine with manipulated hiring and firing policies to increase the adjustment of employment through the external labour market. But firms enact their strategies subject to constraints imposed by the organisation and supply of labour, for which we need a theory of social reproduction.

Although we are in the early stages of developing the micro-economic foundations of this analysis, it is already apparent that, when product and/or labour markets are disturbed (for example, by foreign competition, new technology or social policies), the strategies adopted by capital and labour adapt and the institutional framework changes. Even if there is a well-defined relationship between demand and average unit labour cost, there is unlikely to be a simple and stable relationship between average unit labour cost and employment. Put another way, the magnitude and speed of the response of employment to output change will not be stable parameters, except under special conditions.

The challenge which we must face to design policies to achieve full employment is not simply to find an answer to the question of what is the appropriate macro-economic policy package. If we reject the notion that competition is only about price and cost differences, we need to develop new micro-economic theories which allow for oligopolistic competition and through which we will have to interpret what is meant by full employment.

Notes

[1] See Tarling and Wilkinson (1977).

[2] In a research project financed by the Social Science Research Council on the Economics of Institutionalised Wage Determination.

References

R.J. Ball and E.B.A. St. Cyr (1966) 'Short-term employment functions in British manufacturing industry', Review of Economic Studies.

F.P.R. Brechling (1965) 'The relationship between output and employment in British manufacturing industry', Review of Economic Studies.

C.E.P.G. (1980) Economic Policy Review, April 1980 Volume 6 No. 1, Gower Publishing.

C. Craig, J. Rubery, R. Tarling and F. Wilkinson (1979) 'Abolition and after: the Jute Wages Council', Dept. of Applied Economics, Cambridge, Mimeo.

J. Craig, J. Rubery, R. Tarling and F. Wilkinson (1980) 'Abolition and after: the Cutlery Wages Council', Dept. of Applied Economics, Cambridge, Mimeo.

M.F.W. Hemming and W.M. Corden (1958) 'Import restriction as a instrument of balance of payments policy', Economic Journal.

D. Lal (1979) in Major (1979).

D. Lal (1977) Unemployment and Wage Inflation in Industrial Economies, OECD, Paris.

R.J. Tarling (1980) 'Short-run employment functions: their evolution, failure and replacement', paper presented at a conference on Low pay and labour market segmentation in Berlin.

R.J. Tarling and S.F. Wilkinson (1977) 'The Social Contract: post-war incomes policies and their inflationary impact', Cambridge Journal of Economics.

124

Chart 1 Real wage settlements and money wage increases

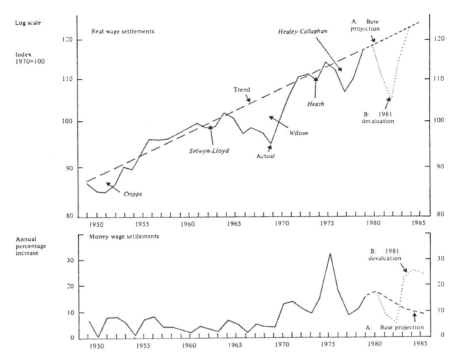

Source: <u>Economic Policy Review</u>, Cambridge, April 1980, p. 26.

MODELS OR MARKETS : TWO APPROACHES TO EMPLOYMENT POLICY*)

Eduard J. Bomhoff, Erasmus University, Rotterdam

I. <u>INTRODUCTION</u>

The first duty of academic economists is not, of course, to tell policymakers what to do, but to spell out the consequences of different policies, so as to raise the level of economic literacy. The aim of this paper is to discuss two quite different ways in which economists can try to fulfill this duty with respect to the current problem of unemployment in the Netherlands. It sets out with a brief review of some important trends in the Dutch economy. After that, section III of the paper considers some examples of the currently dominant way of conducting economic policy. Impressively numerate thanks to heavy reliance on computer simulations with macro-econometric models, this approach is still very rudimentary in modelling economic expectations about the future.

It will be argued that rational individuals do base their behaviour on expectations about the future, and that an econometric model that fails to take this into account is useless as a guide to the conduct of economic policy.

Part IV of the paper attempts once again to discuss some aspects of the unemployment problem, but now from the point of view that an economy consists of rational individuals who try to maximize their utility. The discussion is far from complete; it is restricted to two issues that tend to be neglected in the macro-econometric approach.

First, it deals with ways of reducing the current uncertainty about the future size of the collective burden, and second, with the importance for employment of wage costs, with emphasis not on the average level of wages, as in the macroeconometric approach, but on the structure of relative wages.

The argument in part IV does not rely so much on precise-looking simulations with an econometric model, but on microeconomic reasoning instead and on comparisons with experience in other countries.

*) I am very grateful to Pieter Korteweg for many conversations on the topic of this paper, to Flip de Kam and Roland Vaubel for their comments on the first draft, and to Christian de Boissieu, Angus Maddison and the other participants at the Conference for a spirited discussion.

Table 1

Economic Indicators for Holland and West-Germany, 1973-80

	'73	'74	'75	'76	'77	'78	'79
I Percentage growth rate of industrial production							
Holland	7	5	-5	6	1	1	3
West-Germany	6.5	-1.5	-5.5	8	3	2	5
Difference	0.5	6.5	0.5	-2	-2	-1	-2

II Percentage growth rate of real investment in machinery and equipment

	'73	'74	'75	'76	'77	'78	'79
Holland	14	3.5	-7	-8	18	1.5	3
West-Germany	1	-10	0.5	6.5	7.5	8	10
Ratio (1970=100) (three-year moving average)	101	107	104.5	99.5	95.5	94.5	88.5

III Relative wage costs per unit of output in industry (1970=100)

	'73	'74	'75	'76	'77	'78	'79
Holland./.West-Germany	93	93	101	99	100	98	95.5

IV Collective expenditure as a percentage of gross national product

	'73	'74	'75	'76	'77	'78	'79
Holland	42.5	44.5	48.5	47.5	47.5	49	50.5
West-Germany	36.5	39.5	43.5	42.5	43	42.5	42.5
Difference	6	5	5	5	4.5	6.5	8

Sources :
I, IV : Netherlands Bank, Annual Report for 1979.
II   : Statistisches Bundesamt, Central Planning Bureau and Eurostat
        (European Economy, no. 5, March 1980) for the forecasts.
III   : Central Planning Bureau.

The short concluding section tries to evaluate the relative merits of traditional macroeconometric analysis and an alternative approach which starts from the assumption of rational behaviour by market participants.

II. RECENT ECONOMIC PERFORMANCE - A COMPARISON WITH GERMANY

Table 1 provides some statistics regarding the performance of the Dutch economy during the 1970's. In each part of the table, the figures for Holland are juxtaposed to the corresponding data for the West-German economy. Such a comparison is helpful since it provides a rough and ready way of distinguishing the influence of extraneous events from the effects of domestic polities. Unexpected changes in the relative price of oil and other material inputs or structural changes in the relationship between the O.E.C.D. countries should affect countries in a similar way. Any differences between develpments in Holland and in West-Germany must then be attributed mainly to domestic factors in the two countries.

The first part of table 1 compares the rates of growth of industrial production in the two countries. The data show a consistent excess of Dutch over German growth during the first half of the 1970's. After 1975, however, industrial production in Holland grew more slowly than in Germany in each year. Moreover, in 1978 and 1979 the growth of industrial production in Holland was least of the nine major O.E.C.D. economies[1].

A large part of the year-to-year movements in the growth differential between Holland and Germany can be explained by unexpected aggregate demand shocks in the two countries[2], but there is also a clear longer-run trend which shows a relative deterioration of the industrial sector in the Netherlands.

The second part of the table gives data for gross fixed capital formation in the two countries. After the recession of the mid-seventies and the subsequent recovery, the ratio of Dutch over German investment stood again at approximately 100 in 1976. Since then, there has been a persistent deterioration in Holland, with a further loss expected for the current year. In the third part of the table, wage costs per unit of output in the two countries are expressed in a common currency. There is a clear improvement in wage cost competitiveness for Holland during the last few years, and this holds not only in relation to West-Germany, but also with respect to the E.E.C. average[3].

The last part of table 1 gives summary data for the collective burden in Holland and West-Germany, expressed as a percentage of gross national product. At the beginning of the decade, the collective sector grew more slowly than in West-Germany, so that the difference between the two countries became smaller. After that, developments in both countries were similar in the mid-seventies, with a sharp increase in the ratio during the recession years 1974 and 1975 and a slight decline between 1975 and 1977. During the last few years, however, the ratio has remained stable in West-Germany, but has started to increase again in the Netherlands. This recent difference between the two countries has to be attributed to mutually reinforcing differential trends in both GNP and in collective expenditure. GNP grew much slower in Holland than in West-Germany (annual growth rates between 1977 and 1979 were 2.0 and 3.9 per cent respectively) whereas collective expenditure increased slightly faster in Holland (mean annual growth rates 3.6 per cent and 3.3 per cent respectively.

Taken together, the data in table 1 bring out one of the central issues in Dutch economic policy : in spite of successful attempts at improving cost competitiveness, economic growth in Holland is less than in West-Germany, so that roughly similar increases in collective expenditure lead to even larger differences in the burden of the collective sector in the two countries.

III A MACROECONOMETRIC MODEL AS ARBITER OF ECONOMIC POLICY THE POLITICIANS AND THEIR MODEL

Having described the problem, I now turn to a discussion of one approach which Dutch policy-makers have followed in attempting to solve it. The analysis obviously does not cover all aspects of the current approach, but it highlights a feature which has been important, and needs to be evaluated. Due to the pioneering efforts of Jan Tinbergen, the first Director of the Central Planning Bureau (CPB), macro-econometric models have for long been important in the preparation of economic policy in the Netherlands. Initially, the CPB used a single model both for short-term unconditional forecasting and for simulations of alternative economic policies, but recently there has been a specialisation : a quarterly model is maintained for short-run forecasts, and a new annual model is used for the evaluation of longer-term government policy. Since our concern is economic policy, the analysis that follows will concentrate on the workings of this so-called VINTAF-model[3]. More attention has been paid to this model than to all the earlier econometric efforts of the CPB. The explanation is not to be found on the supply side of the market for econometric models, since the construction of such models has remained but one of the many activities of CPB. A significant shift has occurred, however, on the demand side with perpetual, nervous requests of politicians for new forecasts. By contrast to the U.K., where the Treasury model has become more popular because of an increase in interest from the private sector, in Holland it is the political class which goes ever more frequently to the CPB for answers to its questions. The question thus arises : why have the politicians made VINTAF the arbiter of economic policy?

The popularity of VINTAF can be explained by considering some of the features of the model. In the first place, VINTAF neglects the consequences of government deficits : there are no stocks of money and government debt in the model. Government borrowing is free, and the burden of collective expenditure is measured solely by visible taxes and by social security contributions. Accepting this way of measuring the burden of the collective sector is tantamount to assuming persistent fiscal illusion[4]. This suits politicians fine since it means, to mention but one example, that the government can borrow and use the proceeds to lower social security contributions. Wage costs are reduced in frictionless way, and the model duly predicts an increase in the demand for labour. Apparently, we can bribe ourselves with our own money.

A second characteristic of the VINTAF-model which politicians like is its treatment of business investment. The main determinant of business investment is the average stream of after-tax profits over the past two years. Firms do no try to augment these internally generated funds by borrowing when they are optimistic about the future; neither do companies decide to reduce their real domestic investment when there are good reasons to be pessimistic. No, instead of weighing expected costs against expected benefits, they mechanically invest a certain proportion of their internally available funds.

The way in which investment decisions are modelled in the VINTAF-model has obvious consequences for what that model tells us about the way in which government can try to foster investment. All the incentive effects of lower business taxes are neglected, because there are no real rates of return in the model. Moreover, a reduction in taxes affects investment with a long lag, because both the direct effect on disposable profits and the indirect effect through the accelerator mechanism have to work their way through the 1 year lag in the investment equation. On the other hand, direct subsidies are favoured by this model as a means to stimulate investment. In simulations with the model, the amount of the subsidy is simply added to the right-hand-side of the investment equation. There is no crowding-out, so that a one-guilder subsidy leads to a one-guilder increase in investment.

The built-in preference of the model for direct subsidies is generally shared by politicians, since subsidies provide the more visible means of supporting industry.

A third feature of simulations with the VINTAF-model is due not so much to any deficiencies of that model, but to the specific use to which it is put at the politicians' request. Gross nominal wages are endogenous in the model, but the CPB is asked to calculate the consequences of so-called autonomous decreases in nominal wages. In order to show these effects, the error term in the wage equation is set at some negative value for one or more periods. Consequently, the rate of increase of nominal wages becomes more or less an exogenous variable. "The CPB can have its doubts about this, because of the influence of market forces, but cannot deny that it is a possibility"[6]. The model duly shows strong positive effects of the decrease in wage costs on employment.

Politicians use the simulations as supporting evidence for wage controls. They must share the doubts of the CPB Director, but in case market forces do act to restore real wages to their equilibrium level after the wage freeze has ended, then the failure of the controls can always be conveniently blamed on the labour unions.

Models versus Markets

All three examples of economic policies described above have actually been tried in recent years. Increases in taxes and social security have been kept below the increases in collective expenditure, so that collective goods could apparently be provided below cost. Also, the government has tried to reduce wage costs, both by temporary deferral of increases in social security contributions, and through incomes policies. Dutch cost competitiveness has indeed improved, but none of the favourable effects on economic growth that should have appeared by now, have yet materialised[7]. Finally, the

authorities have shifted from tax incentives to direct
subsidisation of industry, and are even attempting to use the
subsidies as an instrument of counter-cyclical policy[8].
However, business enthusiasm is not universal[9].

Apparently, the model does not reflect reality, since the
market refuses to react according to the model's simulations.

Two opposite hypotheses can provide an explanation for the
apparent pessimism of the market with respect to the future of
Dutch industry. On the one hand it is possible that such
pessimism has to be explained by non-economic, e.g.
psychological factors, and that the government has a
psychological rather than an economic problem on its hands.
Discussion of this hypothesis is better left to the
psychologists. On the other hand market pessimism may be based
on an assessment of the economic situation that is more
realistic than that provided by the model simulations. I shall
review the three examples of economic policies that were
mentioned before, and try to show that each policy may look
fine on the computer print-out, but will make rational economic
agents more pessimistic abut the future.

Increases in government debt, changes from tax incentives
to direct investment subsidies, and incomes policies have one
thing in common : they tend to increase the degree of
uncertainty about the future. For the case of increases in
debt, this has been forcefully put by Parkin : [10].

> "The deficits which have accumulated since 1975 now
> aggregate 38 billion guilders. Assuming an interest
> rate of only 2 percent in real terms, taxes will
> have to be higher forever (unless future surpluses
> offset these deficits) by 760 million guilders per
> annum... If the deficit continues at its current
> rate for as long as another five years, then taxes
> will have to be increased forever by some 2
> billion guilders above what they otherwise would
> have been... Such taxation increases in prospect
> must give pause to anyone contemplating medium-term
> investment plans. Worse, if it is anticipated that
> at some stage in the medium term government
> expenditures are going to be out, then major
> uncertainty surrounds the areas and directions in
> which the cuts will occur and the effects that they
> will have on profitability in various sectors of
> the economy. It is likely that this major source of
> uncertainty is doing major and permanent damage
> both to the long-term growth prospects and the
> detailed allocation of new capital resources".

The reason why incomes policies increase uncertainty are equally obvious : no-one knows when they will be terminated, what will happen then and whether they will be imposed again, possibly in conjunction with restrictions on product prices and dividends.

Changes from tax incentives to direct subsidies for business likewise lead to more uncertainty because they increase the element of discretion in the hands of the politicians and their officials who execute industrial policy. Entrepreneurs may have to "climb the backstairs of politics and administration as the only path to success" and so waste the "treasure of energy" about which Schumpeter speaks.

Rational economic agents will judge economic policy by its long-run effects, and these are less favourable then the model suggests for each of the policies described above. For not only does uncertainty about the future increase, which by itself has a negative effect on output, on top of that each measure has further negative consequences, which do not appear in the VINTAF-model, but are real enough nevertheless. Government borrowing leads to crowding-out in the capital markets. Econometric models which do take crowding-out into account show that a debt-financed increase in government expenditure displaces an equivalent amount of private expenditure[11].

Shifts from tax concessions to more discretionary direct subsidies for business investment also have unfavourable effects in my view, since tax concessions reduce effective taxes on profits and thus strenghten the profit motive, whereas higher taxes combined with direct subsidies imply a larger net burden on the successful and thus a weakening of incentives. Finally, incomes policies may have some favourable effects on inflation in the short run but at the same time obstruct the working of the labour market as employers are prevented from bidding labour away from less to more productive uses. Current Dutch econometric models do not have any room for the negative effects of an ill-functioning labour market (I return to this issue below) and therefore gloss over the serious damage that would be done in my opinion by making the labour market even more distorted and inflexible than it is at present.

The Proper Role of Macro-economometric Models

The hypothesis that economic agents form their expectations rationally can explain the puzzling paradox of Dutch economic policy: a weakening of our industrial strength when compared to West-Germany, although cost competetiveness is improving. Recent government policy has made rational agents both more pessimistic and more uncertain about the future. For, the increases in government debt have to be paid for by higher taxes, the upward trend in the collective burden has to be reversed some time, incomes policy may break down or may on the contrary be strenghtened by a freeze on prices and dividends, and direct subsidies for investment are more likely to be changed frequently than support for business through tax incentives.

If the argument that agents are rational is correct, what conclusions follow for the use of econometric models as a guide to the conduct of economic policy? First, the reason why politicians continuously want policy advice from nonrational macroeconometric models is not their desire to raise the debate about economic policy to a more objective, numerate level, but because the built-in bias in such models corresponds nicely to their own. Second, even if non-rational models are modified with more attention given to monetary phenomena, to "suppply side economics", to the transmission mechanism etc., they still cannot succeed in capturing the essence of the game that is being played between the government and the private sector. For, each move by the government leads the private sector to speculate about whether it will be of a temporary or a permanent nature, whether the change in policy is isolated or just the first in a series of similar measures. Existing econometric models cannot cope with this, since thay reflect some average of the decisions that agents took during the period of estimation, when there was a certain mix between permanent and trasitory, single and repeated shocks to the economy. A systematic change in economic policy means a change in this average mix, and therefore a change in agents' decision rules[12]. Finally, the primary role of econometric models is as a vehicle for testing and advancing macroeconomic theory. It is important for that reason to include monetary phenomena, "supply side economics", a transmission mechanism etc.[13], even though the models will remain useless for simulating changes in economic policy.

IV. ECONOMIC POLICY UNDER RATIONAL EXPECTATIONS: REDUCING UNCERTAINTY

Although macro-econometric models are an unreliable guide for economic policy, that does not mean that we have to search into the night for the lost elixir of economic prosperity. Instead, we must look again at the data in table 1, but this time through the eyes of a rational economic agent, who has to make his decisions in a stochastic and uncertain environment. If such a rational agent studies the figures over the past few years for the collective burden in part IV of the table, then he will forecast a stable collective sector in West Germany and further growth in collective expenditure in Holland. But, since the collective sector can hardly be expected to usurp all of GNP, he must also predict major changes in Dutch policy at some time in the near future.

Anxiety about the future size of the collective sector, is not necessarily the only reason for the weakening of our industrial sector with respect to Germany where the situation is more favourable in these respects [14]. However, it does affect the private sector for at least two reasons. First, the kind of government-induced uncertainty about which Michael Parkin wrote, depresses investment. Second, the "wedge" between gross wages and disposable wages affects employment. Gross wage costs are the correct argument in the demand for labour, but disposable wages in the labour supply function. Thus, a reduction in the wedge will have a favourable effect on employment and profitability in the Dutch private sector[15].

To see why a reversal of the increasing trend in collective expenditure can well have major effect on employment, consider the position of a hypothetical firm which has the choice of investing in Holland or in Germany. Assume that the time horizon of the investment project is ten years and that the firm predicts a continuation of present trends in the size of the collective burden. In that case, the relevant comparison is not between the current figures of 50 per cent in Holland and 42 per cent in Germany (difference : 8), but between an average of 58 per cent in Holland versus 42 per cent in Germany (difference : 15). Once the market assumes that the burden of the collective sector has been stabilized in Holland also, the average figure for Holland decreases from 58 to 50 per cent. Whether the Dutch economy can permanently sustain such a collective burden is another important matter, but there can be little doubt that an end to the rising trend would by itself have a momentous impact on expectations and thus on the propensities to save and invest.

The current trend in collective expenditure not only causes uncertainty about the future and an increasing wedge between gross wages and net wages, but also means that employers have to pay a premium to induce young workers to accept the risks of private sector employment. This risk premium then leads to a further negative effect on employment in the private sector. Policies to re-vitalize Dutch industry stand a better chance of success if they are combined with policies designed to make more young people opt for the training that leads to jobs in the private sector. For that reasong, a negative wage-round in the collective sector can be advocated not only because it leads to a permanent reduction in the collective burden, but also because it increases the attractions of a career in the private sector.

There are many other ways, of course, in which economies can be made, and economists can help to point out the consequences of each cut for the behaviour of market participants, so that the political debate on which cuts to make is well-informed. Here, I want to stress one further favourable consequence of a reversal in the increase of the collective burden : it will become much easier to pursue monetary and fiscal policies that will create a stable and predictable framework for free wage negotiations in the private sector.

Once again it is appropriate to juxtapose the Dutch and the German experience. In Germany, the authorities set a target for inflation through their monetary policy, and leave it to the social partners to agree about increases in nominal wages. In Holland, monetary policy is less predictable in as far as it is largely a derivative of the exchange rate policy of the Dutch Central Bank and on top of that it has to be conducted under a constant risk of being thrown off course by the government's lack of fiscal dicipline. Moreover, current Dutch wage levels poorly reflect the underlying supply and demand factors in the labour market, because of heavy government intrusion in the wage negotiations. It is uncertain whether there will be a continuation of the present incomes policy, or whether market forces will restore wages to their equilibrium

level, which itself depends on uncertain future government
policies with respect to the social security system.

The German authorities try actively to foster a consensus
of expectations about the general short-run prospects of the
economy. Having thus created an efficient framework for the
actual wage negotiations, the authorities leave it to employers
and unions to negotiate about the terms of the wage contract.

The situation in Holland is quite different. Ministers do
not limit their efforts to achieving a consensus of
expectations about the future of the economy, and leave the
practical consequences for wages to those directly concerned;
they simply quote a number for the increase in real wages which
they would prefer, and combine this with threats of wage
controls if the private sector does not oblige. That creates
unnecessary uncertainty about the future course of wages and
prices. Moreover, the evidence from Germany and Switzerland
shows that, as long as agents can easily form accurate
expectations about future government policy, free wage
bargaining does not cause "wage explosions"[16].

The policy framework that has proved successful in Germany
and Switzerland is conducive to reducing uncertainty about the
future. In Holland, too, low and stable rates of increase in
prices and wages would have favourable effects on efficiency
and economic growth and thus (ceteris paribus) on equilibrium
employment[17].

One important element in such a stable framework, namely a
constant growth rule for the money supply, is worth trying in
Holland also, since there exists a stable demand for money
function that can be used to deduce the expected rate of Dutch
price inflation from a publicly announced rate of growth for
the money supply[18].

A reduction of the collective burden, more life chances
for the private sector, stability in monetary and fiscal
policy, and free wage bargaining have for a long time been
advocated by neo-classical economists. It is interesting to
note, however, that some opponents of neo-classical or
monetarist economics have recently changed their counter-

strategy. Instead of arguing for the opposite policies, viz. further increases in the collective burden, less room for the private sector, more discretionary monetary and fiscal policies and heavier government influence over wage negotiations, they now misconstrue monetarism to imply that stable monetary growth will solve each and every economic problem, and claim, by contrast, that their "main reasoning start(s) where the monetarists still usually stop"[19].

A rational expectations approach certainly leads to caution as regards the kind of policies that can easily be simulated with macroeconometric models. On the other hand, the concomitant search for equilibrium theories of the ways in which markets work, cannot but lead to the investigation of policies to change the working of these markets, especially when pressure groups or earlier government policies have been causes of distortions. The remainder of this part of the paper will be devoted to a discussion of some distortions in the Dutch labour market and possible means of lowering the natural unemployment rate by removing these.

Distortions in the Labour Market

The official Dutch VINTAF-model can hardly be faulted for failing to emphasize the importance of real wages for employment. On the contrary : "In this theory the relation between wage cost increases and augmentation of unemployment is closest"[20].

However, attention is directed solely to the average level of real wages, and the model does not allow for the possibility that the structure of wages has anything to do with the unemployment problem. Public discussion of the unemployment problem tends to concentrate also on the relation between average wage costs and unemployment, and to overlook the possibility of serious distortions in the wage structure.

In order to discuss the question whether distortions in the structure of relative wages help to explain the present conditions in the Dutch labour market, we shall need some rudimentary assumptions about the way in which unions and employers decide about wage levels. Let us first of all assume that private sector firms and unions negotiate about the wage level and employment in a situation of uncertainty, both with respect to the future demand schedule faced by the firm, and with respect to the general price level. Under these circumstances an efficient labour contract will leave the determination of the level of employment to the firm[21]. This assumption is important as it provides an equilibrium explanation why unforeseen shifts in demand do not automatically lead to lower real wages with unchanged employment, but rather may cause a fall in employment. We add two stylized assumptions to the Hall-Lilien model : first, labour contracts delegate the administrative function of assigning workers to employment or unemployment to the employer. Second, labour productivity and reliability is not the same for each worker, but cannot be observed directly by the employer. Both assumptions are common in recent equilibrium theorizing about labour contracts[22].

The literature cited above shows that our assumptions so far provide an explanation of unemployment with full wage flexibility and a natural rate of unemployment that may be higher for some categories of workers than for others. They do not yet offer an economic explanation for the recent increases in the natural rates of unemployment for many groups in the Dutch labour market. For that, we require one further assumption, namely that the present relative structure of wages corresponds less to differences in average productivity of the different categories of worker than it did in the past.

There are at least three reasons why union leaders may have worked harder for such a standardization of relative wages, why employers have not resisted this process more, and why public opinion has concurred. In the first place, standardization of wages becomes more likely when its costs are reduced. This has certainly been the case in the Netherlands, where the social security system has become more comprehensive over time. Older workers, for example, have fewer incentives today to organize themselves and protest against union policies that price them out of their jobs through refusing lower wage costs for workers near the retirement age.

Second, the incentive to press for standardization of wages on the part of the prime-age waorkers has increased with the slowing down of the rate of economic growth during the 1970's. One implication of slower economic growth, is fewer opportunities for promotion, so that it becomes more important for the prime-age union members to press for early retirement of older workers. One way to achieve that goal is to keep wages for older workers as high as is feasible.

Finally, public opinion has been keen on equality of income for different groups of workers. This public preference has not been directed so much towards greater equality in total incomes over the life-cycle with its consequences for the financing of higher education and the availability of adult education and re-training. Pressure has been directed rather towards more equality in current wages for different groups of workers. In that way public opinion has provided support for attempts by union leaders to achieve greater standardization.

Wright has stressed the importance of union power for an explanation of contemporary unemployment patterns in Britain :
"Collective agreements themselves involve the establishment of grades, and in some cases the desire of unions to protect their position involves further standardization. Thus, for example, there was no question of older workers being paid less and the wage rates of juveniles were kept high to prevent their becoming cheap substitutes for adult labour. The natural consequence of standardization was that the value to the employer of many employees (actual and potential) did not match the grades, and such employees were not engaged or tended to become redundant... Such policies by firms and unions tended to separate the labour market into two parts : the one comprising the regular employees of large firms, ... the other a collection of residual categories...."[23].

I submit that union domination by prime age males together with the provisions of the social security system and the preference for greater equality in currently earned incomes provides the main explanation of unemployment in Holland. Empirical tests of this proposition could be designed, for example by investigating whether wage differentials between the different age groups are less in industries with strong unions. My cursory review of the literature has not uncovered any such tests for the Dutch economy. The Dutch government, to be sure, accepts the relevance of the hypothesis :

"The friction in the labour market is caused partly
because the structure of wages acts as a hindrance
to the employment of specific disadvantaged
groups"[24].

Micro-economic Policies for the Labour Market

Trade unions perform important functions, for example in
insuring their members against individual acts of injustice on
the part of employers, and because they can lower information
costs in the labour market. For these and other reasons, I
disregard the option of trying to solve the imperfections in
the wage structure by prohibiting collective agreements between
unions and employers. Fortunately, at least two other
approaches for improving the labour market remain :
1) making the social security system less generous, so
that both workers who presently receive social security
and employed persons withh lower-than average human
capital will exert greater pressure on the employed
workers in the primary groups to prevent real wages from
becoming too high for them. In this way, average real
wages can be expected to fall and employment to increase.
Consequently the collective burden will decrease, as
collective expenditure goes down, while GNP goes up. This
may be expected to have further positive
2) introducing a system of targeted employment subsidies
for certain categories of disadvantaged workers in order
to correct the structure of wages and to make it feasible
for recipients of social security to compete again in the
labour market.

Option (1) across the board cuts in social security, has
the disadvantage of hurting those recipients who do not have a
free choice between working and not-working, for example the
severely disabled. Option (2) would on that score be preferable
if it could be made to work. I shall devote the remainder of
this section to arguing that option (2) is indeed worth
trying.

Categorical employment subsidies have been discussed in
the economic literature for some time, and have found many
advocates [25]. A concrete application to the Dutch situation

could, for example, be some form of the "voucher plan" for all recipients of disability benefits : each permanently disadvantaged person receiving a voucher which has no direct value to him, but which can be handed over to any employer who is willing to employ the bearer. The voucher entitles the employer to a subsidy, either direct or in the form of reduced social security contributions, for as long as he employs the disadvantaged worker at the going wage.

The crucial element in this proposal is that the subsidy is permanent. Until now, the Dutch government has categorically rejected the ideal of permanent subsidies, because it appears to deny the existence of permanent disadvantages in the labour market:[26]

The voucher plan would enable recipients of disability benefits to compete in the labour market, so that real wages would fall and employment could increase. The scheme has possible adverse displacement effects[27]. However - as pointed out by Layard and Nickell - displacement is less in a small, open economy. Also the vouchers will have strong favourable first round effects on collective expenditure, with further positive effects on the demand for labour[28].

Another possibility is dispensation from the minimum youth wage for those employers who offer substantial job training, together with a "youth employment scholarship" paid to trainees as a supplement to their wage income.
According to Feldstein:
"Unfortunately, the current minimum wage law prevents many young people from accepting jobs with low pay but valuable experience ... Note that this view of the harmful effects of applying the minimum wage law ... is quite different from the usual proposition that the minimum wage law creates unemployment because at the established level the supply of workers exceeds the demand. The evidence on that is ambiguous. The important point is that, because of the minimum wage law, many of the jobs that are available do not provide young workers and their employers with an incentive for stable employment..."[29].

Empirical research has supported Feldstein's hypothesis for the United States[30].

A study of youth unemployment in Britain on the one hand (where unions have exerted a strong influence on minimum wages and conditions of work for youth) and West-Germany, Switzerland and Austria on the other hand (where employers have more leeway in offering training schemes) provides further support[31]. The recent request by a Dutch federation of employers for just this policy, suggests that the situation in Holland is similar[32]. Dispensation from the minimum youth wage for those Dutch employers who offer job training schemes should – on the basis of this evidence – certainly be granted.

An important feature of both proposals is that they rely on self-selection for the identification of their beneficiaries[33]. The principle of self-selection is important as it improves the allocative efficiency of redistribution programs; self-selection has to be preferred, wherever possible, as a more efficient alternative to bureaucratic decision-making.

Taken together, micro-economic policies, such as those described above, should reduce the high natural rates of unemployment for many groups of workers that have been caused by a combination of union pressure, an extensive social security system and the stress on greater equality in current incomes.

V. Conclusions

There has been a growing consensus in the Netherlands that the "enormous treasure of energy" to be found in the private sector of the economy[34].

This paper has been concerned with the question how economists can be of most help in locating and raising this treasure. After a brief sketch of some recent macroeconomic trends, the body of the paper attempted to contrast two alternative research strategies. First, some examples were given of the currently dominant approach, with its heavy reliance on simulations with the official Dutch macroeconometric model. It was argued that the present generation of macroeconometric models is still seriously flawed and unreliable as a guide to economic policy because these models fail to incorporate the role which expectations play in determining economic behaviour.

The macroeconometric approach has additional costs since it tends to obscure potentially important issues simply because the model is incapable of handling them. Two such issues were discussed as examples of an alternative approach to economic policy, which starts from the assumption that economic agents are rational maximizers and tries to investigate the way in which markets work in the real world. First, one important, but oft neglected characteristic of the economic environment was evaluated, namely the uncertainty under which firms and consumers have to make their plans about the future. The current generation of macroeconometric models has nothing to say about the effects of more or less uncertainty on economic decision making, but that does not mean that governments can do nothing to reduce it. Anxieties about the future size of the collective burden depend in a very direct way on government policies, and the authorities can also foster greater predictability about future prices by pursuing stable monetary and fiscal policies.

In the second place, some features of the Dutch labour market were discussed. Once again, the analysis was concerned with issues that are completely neglected by the official model. The failure of wages to reflect differences in productivity was postulated as a major cause of high natural rates of unemployment for many groups in the labour market. Arguments were presented why this phenomenon has become more severe in recent years, and two policies were mentioned that could reduce the resultant rise in unemployment. One possible policy would be a system of permanent vouchers for handicapped workers, so as to enable them to compete again in the labour market. The second change in policy that was discussed consisted of the abolition of the minimum youth wage in order to make it more attractive for companies to offer apprenticeships to young persons. This measure could be combined with income-support programs for the apprentices, but the cost of such programs would have to be paid out of taxes, and not by the employers.

The arguments in this section of the paper could not be supported with econometric simulations. The paper will have achieved its purpose if that is not seen as a great handicap and if it can be agreed that equilibrium economics, that is : economics based on the assumption of rational behaviour, has much (if only in more competent hands than those of the present author) to contribute to the analysis of unemployment.

Notes

1] Annual Report of the Dutch Central Bank, 1979, Statistical Annex, table 11.2.

2] E.J. Bomhoff, Inflation, the Quantity Theory, and Rational Expectations, North-Holland, Amsterdam, 1980, chapter 4.

3] See CPB, Centraal Economisch Plan 1980, p. 47 : "a remarkable improvement in competitiveness during the last few years". According to the CPB, this remains true if allowance is made for differences between countries in the composition of exports.

4] H. den Hartog et.al., Een macro model voor de Nederlandse economie op middellange termijn, CPB Occasional Paper no. 12, 1977.

5] Money illusion : the assumption that agents are unable to separate "real" from "nominal" economic news; fiscal illusion: the assumption that agents are incapable of assessing the future consequences of current government deficits.

6] C.A. van den Beld "Het Centraal Planbureau : zijn invloed, zijn macht en zijn onmacht" in : W.M. van den Goorbergh et.al., Over macht en wet in het economisch gebeuren, Opstellen aangeboden aan prof. dr. D.B.J. Schouten, Stenfert Kroese, Leiden, 1979, 50-75.

7] Both the VINTAF-model and the quarterly model indicate short mean lags of no more than one year for the influence of a change in cost competetiveness in the equation for exports.

8] Financieel Dagblad, May 29, 1980:
"The basic subsidy for investment in machinery will be temporarily increased from 7 to 10 per cent... According to Prime Minister Van Agt, this measure is intended to be counter-cyclical and aims to improve the low rate of investment... The increase is to be financed by way of lowering the subsidy on investment in buildings...".

9] Trouw, May 29, 1980, reports that the chairmen of the federation of employers in mechanical and electrical engineering has expressed his "Strong aversion to subsidies".

10] J.M. Parkin, "The economy of the United Kingdom", in : J.M. Parkin et.al., Policy Statement and Position Papers for the 1977 meeting of the Shadow European Economic Policy Committee, University of Rochester : Graduate School of Management, 1977. (The quotation is from page 19; I have changed his numerical example to fit the Dutch data).

11] P. Minford, "The Nature and Purpose of U.K. Macroeconometric Models", Three Banks Review, March 1980, 3-26, contrasts results for three Keynesian models and for two rational expectations models of the U.K. economy.

12] R.E. Lucas and T.J. Sargent, "After Keynesian Macro-economics", in : After the Phillips Curve : Persistence of High Inflation and High Unemployment, Federal Reserve Bank of Boston, 1978, 49-72; E.J. Bomhoff, Inflation, the Quantity Theory and Rational Expectations, chaper 5.

13] See, for example, A. Knoester, Over Geld en Economische Politiek, Stenfert Kroese, Leiden, 1980.

14] A number of other hypotheses about the relative decline of Dutch industry is discussed briefly in E.J. Bomhoff, "Het CPB en de economische politiek", Economisch Statistische Berichten, July 2, 1980.

15] See P. Korteweg, "The Economics of Stagflation : Theory and Dutch Evidence", Zeitschrift für die gesamte Staatswissenschaft, December 1979, 553-583; K.B. Leffler, "Government output and National Income Estimates", Journal of Monetary Economics, Supplement no. 9, 233-266.

16] Holland had a single "wage explosion" in 1963-'64, but that episode can be adequately explained by economic factors; see E.J.Bomhoff, "Het CPB en de loonexplosie van 1964", Tijdschrift voor politieke economie, February 1978. As noted there, the CPB has never had to introduce a dummy variable in its wage equations to account for the increase in wages in that year.

17] See P. Korteweg, "The Economics of Stagflation: Theory and Dutch evidence", Zeitschift für die gesamte Staatswissenschaft, December 1979, 553-583. Korteweg shows empirically that increased uncertainty about future relative prices (itself a consequnce of higher and more variable rates of inflation) has significant effects on real output.

18] See P. Korteweg, "The Economics of Stagflation" Op.cit.;
E.J. Bomhoff, Inflation, the Quantity Theory and Rational
Expectations, Chapter 4. Constant money growth wuld be
feasible only if the determination of the exchange rte
between the guilder and the DMark were left to the market.
Two additional arguments for such a change in policy are :
first, it is easier to cover exchange risk in the forward
currency market than to cver the risks of prediction
errors with respect to domestic inflation, which is what
risk averse residents would be concerned about most.
Second, a Central Bank that tries to fix the exchange rate
may try to peg it for too long at an inappropriate value,
for example if the Bank fails to recognize shifts in the
equilibrium value of the real exchange rate.

19] G. Rehn, interview in Challenge, July-August 1980, 42-46.

20] P.J.L.M. Peters, "Wage costs and labour demand with some
reference to employment in the Netherlands", De Economist,
124, no. 1/2, 18-32.

21] R.E. Hall and D.M. Lilien : Eficient wage bargains under
uncertain supply and demand, American Economic Review,
December 1979, 868-879. The statement in the text depends
on a (plausible) assumption about the relative variances
of demand and supply shocks.

22] For example, H.I. Grossman, "Risk shifting, layoffs, and
seniority", Journal of Monetary Economics, November 1978,
661-686.

23] J.F. Wright, Britain in the Age of Economic Management :
An Economic History since 1939, Oxford University Press,
1979, p. 104. About the postulated domination of union
policies by prime age members see also J.L. Medoff,
"Layoffs and Alternatives under Trade Unions in U.S.
Manufacturing", American Economic Review, June 1979, 380-
395 and M. Olson, "The political biases of Keynesian
Economics, Comments in : J.M. Buchanan and R.F. Wagner,
eds., Fiscal Responsability in Constitutional Democracy,
Martinus Nijhoff, Leiden and Boston, 1978, 106-117.

24] Bestek '81, Tweede kamer no. 15081, 1978, p. 163.

25] See, for example, Brookings Papers on Economic Activity, 1976, no. 1, p. 113-114 for statements of support by Tobin, Feldstein and R.J. Gordon. The most extensive singel source of information is : J.L. Palmer, Creating Jobs - Public Employment Programs and Wage Subsidies, Brookings Institution, 1978, in particular the articles or comments by Hamermesh, Gramlich, Lerman, Wiseman, and Kemper-Moss. The papers in this volume show that wage subsidies are more efficient than public employment under a variety of assumptions, with a possible exception for the most disadvantaged workers only.

26] See Nota inzake de werkgelegenheid, Tweede Kamer nr. 13318, 1975, p. 67-68; Bestek '81, p. 163: "To apply such measures (wage subsidies, E.J.B.) permanently, would go against the principle of fair competition and would imply a suboptimal use of factors of production".

27] See, for example, P.R.G. Layard and S.J. Nickell, "The case for subsidising extra jobs", Economic Journal, March 1980, 51-73.

28] For the first-round effects, see S. Mukherjee, Government and Labour Markets, P.E.P., London, 1976; C.A. de Kam, "Recessie en economische groei", Socialisme en democratie, September, 1975, 388-405. Currently no more than one per cent of the recipients of disability payments succeed in becoming re-employed.

29] M.S. Feldstein, "The Economics of the New Unemployment", Public Interest, Fall 1973, 3-42.

30] J. Mincer and L. Leighton, The effects of Minimum Wages on Human Capital Formation, N.B.E.R., Working Paper no. 441, 1980.

31] See J. Grimond, ed., Youth Unemployment and the Bridge from School to Work, Anglo-German Foundation, London, 1980.

32] See NRC-Handelsblad, June 5, 6, 1980 for the employers' request and an angry, completely irrational reaction from the trade union movement.

33] G.A. Akerlof, "The economics of "tagging" as applied to the optimal income tax, welfare programs, and manpower planning", American Economic Review, March 1978, 8-19.

34] G.A. Kessler, "De publieke sector in de jaren tachtig", Economisch Statistische Berichten, 64, no. 3226, October 17, 1979, 1065-1072 produces the evidence.

COMMENTS ON BOMHOFF'S PAPER

Christian de Boissieu, University of Rouen and University of Paris

E. Bomhoff's paper is a rich and stimulating contribution on the role played by economic policy in recent economic trends in the Netherlands. His argument hinges on the following considerations :

1. For some years now, there has been a tendency towards de-industrialisation in the Netherlands, despite the improved competitive position of the Dutch economy.
2. The macro-economic models favoured by the public authorities suffice neither to explain nor check this trend.
3. De-industrialisation is probably due mainly to the uncertainty generated by economic policy itself and the increase in the collective burden.
4. There are measures that would have the effect of reducing the natural rate of unemployment, the increase in the collective burden and the degree of uncertainty in the economy.

Under the item 2, the author strongly criticises the medium-term model used by the C.P.B., the VINTAF model. The objections levelled at the investment function and the treatment of nominal wages seem to me to be less important and more conventional than those concerning the omission of the impact of public debt and "crowding-out effects". Bomhoff explains brilliantly how the political class in the Netherlands is able via this model to legitimize its preferences and its action. The contrast, which underlies the paper, between the macro-economic models approach and the rational expectations approach is in theory not very convincing; not all macro-economic models eliminate uncertainty and expectations phenomena, while the rational expectations concept is based fundamentally on the model concept.

The contrast does, however, exactly convey Bomhoff's position; the VINTAF model corresponds neither to the "relevant economic theory", nor to the "true" model of the Dutch economy. Bomhoff's scepticism with regard to macro-economic models is at present fairly widely shared. It is sufficient by way of illustration to recall the criticisms that economists have levelled at the main American macro-economic models. I leave it to the specialists to assess the VINTAF model, and will lay stress on the three other topics discussed.

I. A few comments on the diagnosis

De-industrialisation is an ambiguous concept. In tackling it, reference may be made to criteria which are valid however open the economy : percentage of the working population employed in the secondary sector, rate of growth of industrial production, etc. In his classic study, N. Kaldor (1966) emphasized the impact of transfers of labour from the secondary to the tertiary sector on overall economic growth and the trend in average labour productivity. Here, Bomhoff emphasizes the production rather than the employment criterion. De-industrialisation is observed by means of inter-temporal comparisons (slowdown in the growth of industrial production and of gross fixed capital formation; expansion of the public sector role) and inter-spatial comparisons (the Federal Republic of Germany serves as a "standard", but differences in the average propensities to import need to be incorporated in the reasoning).

According to the reasoning, de-industrialisation also corresponds to a situation in which the growth of industrial production drops below the growth of GDP (as in the Netherlands between 1977 and 1979). Industrial production curbs overall economic growth instead of acting as a stimulus. In the case of an economy as open as that of the Netherlands, it would seem essential to supplement the internal criteria with criteria which are valid in an open economy. To take the example of the work by A. Singh (1977) with regard to the United Kingdom, it is important to consider the share of Dutch industrial production in the domestic and international markets, and also the trend in the trade balance of Dutch industry. Reference should have been made to some of the criteria of the Cambridge School; this would have supplemented and perhaps qualified Bomhoff's findings. The author refers to the favourable trend in unit labour costs compared with the Federal Republic of Germany and the other EEC countries. As has already been emphasized by C.A. van den Beld (1979), however, the Dutch example confirms the absence of a direct connection between export performance and trends in unit costs. The terms of trade do not always accurately reflect production costs, and the differences between the two series are liable to be wider in sectors exposed to international competition than in protected sectors.

II. Rate of de-industrialisation and degree of uncertainty

Bomhoff's thinking is along the same lines as the work of Bacon and Eltis (1976). Like them, he stresses the "crowding-out effects" engendered by the growth in collective expenditure and the public debt : the expansion of the public sector has a negative influence on the growth of industry.

However, Bomhoff extricates himself from the logic, and in some cases even the trap, of the accounting relations underlying the approach used by Bacon and Eltis. In the opinion of the latter, the growth of the non-market sector combines two unfavourable effects : it assumes a transfer of production factors from the market to the non-market sector (the supply side effect), and it increases the proportion of production by the market sector used outside this sector (the demand side effect). Bomhoff is wary of the arithmetic of Bacon and Eltis, and half opens the Pandora's box of expectations. It is tempting to turn to rational expectations, made pessimistic by growing uncertainty, and this no doubt partly explains recent trends. The value of the analysis lies in making expectations (concerning prices, nominal wages, etc.) endogenous : they are shaped mainly by the expected growth of collective expenditure and the anticipation of this or that economic policy measure. Wage policy, it is suggested, increases uncertainty in that transactors wonder about possible changes and when it will be stopped. These proposals again raise the question of the links between uncertainty and economic policy, and the answers provided by the monetarist school and the theoreticians of rational expectations.

The works by Lucas, Sargent and Wallace show that, on the rational expectations assumption, only the non-systematic component of economic policy (and monetary policy in particular) exerts any influence on production and employment. This work is generally put forward in order to justify the neutralisation of economic policy : since discretionary measures are fully anticipated and therefore thwarted, it is preferable to be satisfied with "rules without feedback", to stabilize and make homogeneous the expectations of private transactors by means of automatic or semi-automatic policies. Bomhoff agrees with these conclusions : Incomes policy must be applied continuously or not at all; the targeted job subsidies suggested by the author must be permanent, etc. In order to reduce uncertainty, it is essential to eliminate the surprise effects arising from economic policy.

This position prompts five observations :
1) The distinction between temporary measures and permanent policy is of differing significance depending on whether it is considered ex ante or ex post:
- a discretionary measure of which the limited period of application is known a priori is often at the root of certain perverse effects (for example, investment projects are delayed pending the introduction of a tax deduction for investments);

- a measure considered <u>ex ante</u> to be permanent may perhaps stabilize the public's expectations but it also gives rise to learning phenomena which reduce its effectiveness;
- in many cases, the effectiveness of a discretionary measure stems from uncertainty as to how long it will be in force, so that the public's "reactive" (or compensatory) behaviour is kept within certain thresholds. Is an economic policy applied continuously always more effective than measures introduced at intervals? The example of credit ceilings in France prompts a qualified answer to this question; while initially discontinuous, credit ceiling policy has been continuous since the end of 1972.

The effectiveness of discontinuous credit ceilings rests on surprise effects, but it has been reduced by the strategic behaviour of the public anticipating the return of credit restrictions. Conversely, the public and the banks have had time to become accustomed to continuous credit ceilings.

2)   A distinction must be made between the standpoint of the private transactor and that of the public authorities. Since Bomhoff adopts the viewpoint of non-State transactors in his analysis, he concludes logically that investment and labour recruitment are encouraged when uncertainty is reduced. From the point of view of public decision-makers, discretionary measures become increasingly effective as the public grows more uncertain. This is the paradoxical lesson to be learned from the theory of rational expectations - paradoxical in that, instead of extolling the merits of permanent and stable economic policies, it recommends random discretionary measures involving intense surprise effects.

3)   The majority of rational expectations models postulate that the behaviour of the government and the public is fundamentally asymmetrical. The government is expected to "take first turn" and not to adopt a strategic behaviour pattern; it does not seek to determine the public's reaction function and is probably alone in the system in not referring to rational expectations. The public, on the other hand, as is well illustrated in Bomhoff's analysis, seeks to anticipate changes in discretionary measures.

4)   Carrying on from the proceding observation, incorporating rational expectations in the theory of economic policy should result systematically in games of strategy, with at least two players (the public authorities and the public), which make the analysis more symmetrical.

Bomhoff briefly suggests such an approach. I personally have referred to game theory in order to propose a conflictual interpretation of Fisher's equation when ceilings on credit result in rationing on the credit market [3]. The monetary authorities endeavour to control the growth of money supply and the public reacts with an increase in the velocity of money.

Game theory still has many limitations. However, the study of games in the extensive form allows rational expectations models to be made symmetrical by analysing how each agent (the public authorities or the public) seeks to discover the reaction function of the other, while at the same time preventing the latter from determining its own reaction function. In the relevant literature, rational expectations are beginning to be discussed in terms of game theory. But it is astonishing that reference to games of strategy should not have been made earlier.

5) In Bomhoff's analysis, rational expectations are somewhat superimposed on the analysis. The author suggests forcefully that the "relevant economic theory" referred to by private transactors in the Netherlands is not written into the VINTAF model. The public is assumed a priori to make efficient use of the information available. However, no details are provided as to the nature of the information available (1), or as to the question of the learning process and the convergence of the estimated model towards the "true" model of the economy.

III. Concerning the measures envisaged in order to reduce the natural rate of unemployment

As it is developed, the argument shifts from production towards employment, without changes in labour productivity being taken into account.

(1) I refer to the distinction made by B. Friedman (1979) between two aspects: the nature of the information available and the way this information is handled.

This is a pity, because de-industrialisation should also be assessed in terms of the trend of labour productivity, and through studying the degree of stability of the link between the rate of growth of productivity and the rate of growth of productivity and the rate of growth of production (this is the standpoint of "Verdoorn's law").

Bomhoff bases his argument on the theories of labour market segmentation, and claims that primary workers impose a wage structure unfavourable to the employment of secondary workers: the wage range would be reduced by unions led by primary workers with the result that, for secondary workers, real wages would be too high in relation to labour productivity.

The measures suggested in order to reduce real wages for secondary workers prompt a number of comments:

1)   The reasoning rests on the assumption that secondary workers are experiencing classical unemployment. According to E. Malinvaud (1977), there must be a drop in real wages for classical unemployment to be reduced and a return to Walras' general equilibrium to be possible. It would be desirable from the economic policy point of view, and delicate from the statistical standpoint, to break down the unemployment of secondary workers into classical and Keynesian unemployment, and to consider the links between these two distinctions: primary and secondary workers; Keynesian and classical unemployment. I doubt whether the unemployment of secondary workers in the Netherlands is solely classical.

		Unemployment	
		Keynesian	Classical
Workers	primary		
	secondary		x

Bomhoff gives priority to the box with a cross. However, this situation does not cover every possible case.
2)   The author levels unqualified criticism at temporary investment subsidies, and expresses himself in favour of permanent targeted job subsidies. The job subsidies suggestion is an old one. Having been previously put forward by Kaldor (1936), it has been taken up again in the last few years by G. Rehn and numerous other authors.
      The desire to set up a permanent and stable system of subsidies has to be linked with monetarist doctrine : the author extends to employment policy the monetarists' preferences for rules without feedback. In contrast with temporary aid to investment, which is a typical example of a rule with feedback (the discretionary measure is altered according to the degree of achievement of the targets), permanent job subsidies belong to semi-automatic economic policy. They are to some extent to employment policy what Friedman's golden rule is to monetary questions. As has been stressed, permanence is an ambiguous criterion: must it be an ex ante subjective certainty, or an objective finding made ex post? To the extent that monetarism has always had a great aversion for selective measures, the highly selective nature of the proposed system means departing from it on this point. It should be added, however, that the degree of tolerance of monetarist thought with regard to selectivity is assumed to be greater in respect of employment (cf. the concept of the natural rate of unemployment and the structural policies suggested in order to reduce it) than in respect of monetary

policy. There can be no question here of reiterating all the discussions concerning the various systems of employment subsidies. Suffice it briefly to discuss a few controversial topics.

a)   It is essential to know the production function applicable and the value of the elasticity of substitution between factors (here, in particular, between secondary workers and other factors of production). Is increased employment obtained at the cost of a reduction in working hours?   Does additional secondary employment reduce primary employment? The experiments carried out in the United States (Eisner, 1980) or in a few European countries do not provide a precise answer.

b)   Does the proposed system prompt an adjustment by prices and/or quantities?   Many supporters of job subsidies consider that reducing the relative cost of labour brings down sale prices and improves the economy's external competitiveness. This "concealed devaluation" would serve to curb de-industrialisation. Others emphasize that job subsidies can give rise to wage increases.

c)   In the Netherlands as elsewhere, job subsidies capable of checking the increase in classical unemployment must be combined with policies for expanding global demand so as to contain the growth of Keynesian unemployment.

3)   The proposed measures consist of job subsidies and exemptions from minimum wage regulations. Obviously there is the question of the budgetary cost and financing of these measures. Those in favour of job subsidies consider their budgetary cost to be low or even nil, job subsidies taking the place of unemployment benefits. Numerical estimates are lacking, however, and Bomhoff does not venture to provide such estimates for the Netherlands. Little is known about the impact of job subsidies on the equilibrium of pulic finance and social finance. It is not sufficient to analyse the difference between job subsidies and the unemployment benefits previously paid to wage-earners recruited as a result of these incentives.   It is equally important to incorporate the effect of job subsidies on economic growth, and hence on social security contributions and tax   receipts.

REFERENCES

R. Bacon et W. Eltis, <u>Britain's Economic Problem</u> : <u>Too Few Producers</u>, Macmillan, London, 1976.

C.A. Van den Beld, "De-industrialisation in the Netherlands?" in F. Blackaby, (ed.), <u>De Industrialisation</u>, Heinemann, London, 1979.

Ch. de Boissieu, <u>Les Vitesses de Circulation de la Monnaie. Une approche conflictuelle</u>, Cujas, Paris, 1975.

R. Eisner, "Incitation à l'emploi plutôt qu'à l'investissement", <u>Revue Economique</u>, January 1980.

B. Friedman, "Optimal Expectations and the Extreme Information Assuptions of "Rations Expectations" Macromodels", <u>Journal of Monetary Economics</u>, January 1979.

N. Kaldor, "Wage Subsidies as a Remedy for Unemployment", <u>Journal of political Economy</u>, December 1936.

N. Kaldor, <u>Causes of the Slow Rate of Economic Growth of the United Kingdom</u>, Cambridge University Press, 1966.

E. Malinvaud, <u>The Theory of Unemployment Reconsidered</u>, Basil Blackwell, 1977.

A. Singh, "U.K. Industry and the World Economy : A Case of De Industrialisation", <u>Cambridge Journal of Economics</u>, June 1977.

THE STRUCTURALIST DIAGNOSIS AND POLICY MENU

Gerhard Willke, Tubingen University and European University Institute, Florence

Introduction

"Structuralists" are people who not only complain about some of the aggregate generalisations of the Keynesian and monetarist schools but do something about it. They treat unemployment and inflation as structural problems, insisting on the relevance of diagnosis at a disaggregated level. Our intention is to emphasize the meso-economic level of analysis, implying that there is a useful level of aggregation between micro and macro. Whereas micro is concerned with 'representative' individual producers or consumers and macro with production or consumption of the economy as a whole, the meso-economic approach considers the behaviour of intermediate aggregates like branches of industry, markets for particular goods or segments of the labour market. Three basic assumptions underly the structuralist approach. First, it assumes that product and labour markets are heterogeneous. The borders of the partial markets are constituted by specific transaction rigidities which, obviously, include price and wage stickiness. Only in models "where excess supplies do not cause reductions in prices and wages" can the simultaneity of excess supplies and inflation be explained (Negishi 1979). We do not imply a strict fixprice model. It is sufficient to postulate that quantities adjust faster than prices - downwardly. Secnd, we assume that disequilibrium transactions do take place and produce the effect of non-price rationing, imposing mutual quantity constraints on product and labour markets. Third, the assumption is that the adaptation of prices and wages to demand and supply, and of quantities to changes in prices, is asymmetrical i.e. non-linear. Excess supplies induce no or negligeable price/ wage reductions whereas excess demands lead to appreciable increases in prices/wages. In fact, asymmetries are held to be a rather general phenomenon in economic and social affairs. The emphasis of this approach is prompted, as usual, by the emergence of a puzzle that can be explained only inadequately by mainstream theories. The puzzle consists in the simultaneity of persistently high or even increasing rates of inflation and unemployment. Neither classical full-employment nor Keynesian unemployment theories are able to deal satisfactorily with it. Where the problem is adressed in 'new microeconomic' terms, unemployment is stylised into voluntary forms which is unhelpful for the situation under consideration, i.e. unemployment rates up to ten percent. Keynes' theory, based on the assumption of homogeneous labour and of the homogeneous macroeconomic state, cannot explain, either, a persistent simultaneity of apparently contradictory market conditions : excess supplies and inflation.

In any explanation of the problem at hand it seems to be necessary to acknowledge the fact of heterogeneous labour and product markets, of asymmetrical price and quantity adaptations, and of mutual quantity constraints between product and labour markets. This will allow us to proceed from the notion of structural equilibrium, usually implied in mainstream approaches, to that of structural disequilibrium – meaning that aggregate imbalances between potential output and effective demand on the one hand, labour supply and demand on the other hand, usually go along with disproportionate imbalances on the disaggregated level of industries and labour market segments, and, more importantly, even in the case of an aggregate balance between supply and demand one would expect disequilibria to continue to exist on that disaggregated level.

The Stylized Facts

The puzzle, as we perceive it, consists of the inadequate explanation by mainstream theories of a number of facts that became particularly salient in the 1970s.

Compared with the decade preceding the 1970s, the rate of unemployment has more than doubled in the European Community, and presently affects more than seven million people.

Again compared with the 1960s, inflation has soared to unheard- of levels, in averaging 12 per cent in the Community in 1980.

Unemployment has become rather inelastic with respect to increases in demand pressure. In many countries, unemployment has not only not declined in cyclical upswings but has either stagnated or even continued to rise. In fact, we have had periods of a simultaneous aggravation of both unemployment and inflation. Even at low levels of capacity utilisation, measures of demand expansion have mostly triggered off inflationary spurts.

The rate of economic growth has declined noticeably from almost 5 per cent in the 1960s to roughly 3 per cent in the 1970s in the EC. As growth is slowing down, structural change is felt much more acutely, even though the rate of change has

not increased. Factors made redundant in declining or stagnant
branches are less readily absorbed for a lack of expanding
branches.

Something has happened to the mixed economic systems after
the unique post-war expansion. Whereas in the 1960s we had
growth, employment and little inflation, in the 1970s we
experienced a dismal combination of unemployment, inflation and
little growth, and the signs of a turn for the better are
lacking.

It has been said that the so-called crisis of the 1970s is
actually closer to normalcy than the years of economic miracles
in the 1950s and 1960s. A Kaleckian 'broken-back economy' with
high inflationary pressure is alleged to be the necessary
outcome of the political economy of advanced capitalist
systems. Whatever the merit of these critiques, they should not
be taken as an argument for resignation. There are, I believe,
good reasons for working at better theories and policies in
face of over 7 million unemployed in the member countries of
the EC.

Inadequacies of Mainstream Theories

One of the great merits of Keynes' theory is that he
rejected the formerly accepted independence between the product
and labour markets, and instead analysed the employment effects
of deficient demand in the aggregate product market. This line
of reasoning is extended in modern disequilibrium theories with
quantity rationing. Keynes' emphasis on the aggregate level and
on the short term, however, has led Keynesians to neglect the
fact that there is no such thing as a homogeneous macroeconomic
state. Similarly, the limitations of the assumption of a non-
evolutionary short-run have been neglected. The structure of
productive capacities and of effective demand are assumed to
remain as unchanged as the composition of the labour force. If
the structures are 'right' and remain so by assumption, then
the unemployment resulting from deficient demand is a purely
quantitative problem. Given invariant patterns of demand,
capacities and labour, a recovery of effective demand is
assumed to perfectly rematch the unemployed with the re-
emerging vacancies.

A weaker interpretation of the Keynesian "state of
suspended animation" (A. Coddington, 1978) is that the changes
that do occur in the short run are quite negligible. This may
be so in the case of a rate of unemployment of 13 per cent in a
cyclical peak year (Britain in 1937) when Keynes advised
retarding the expansion of aggregate demand (see Hutchison

1977). But in the meantime, our full-employment goals have changed, and we can no longer neglect the changes in structure nor the differentiation within the macroeconomic aggregates.

The assumption of a homogeneous macroeconomic state is a prerequisite for the Keynesian hypothesis of a basic trade-off between inflation and unemployment. According to this view, 'the' product market is either characterized by a pervasive deficiency of demand – then we get unemployment and an ensuing decrease of prices and wages – or there is general excess demand relative to a 'normal' degree of capacity utilization, with resulting inflation. It had important consequences that this relation was asserted to be stable, and hence could be used as a basis for policy choices. Although the hypothesis of a trade-off has become discredited, the idea is still around that we would spend our way out of unduly high unemployment at no other cost than a once-and-for-all increase in the rate of inflation. But how can we base our policies on the idea of a trade-off when in reality we have simultaneity of high inflation and unemployment over extended periods?

The idea of a homogeneous macroeconomic state needs to be dropped. If we allow market conditions in the different brances to vary around their macroeconomic mean – which according to Fitoussi (1978, 1979) represents structural deisquilibrium – and if we introduce structural change in addition to fluctuations of aggregate demand, then a necessary argument for a stable trade-off is obviated. If we assume, in conformity with the Keynesian approach, asymmetrical price and wage adjustments in disequilibrium, i.e. downward stickiness, then we would expect inflationary pressures in the relatively expanding branches and quantity adjustments, i.e. redundancies in the relatively stagnating branches : The assumed trade-off between inflation and unemployment turns into a simultaneity.

Monetarist theorizing has been sceptical of the Phillips-curve trade-off on the grounds that the original concept disregarded the difference between nominal and real magnitudes, and that only in the case of unanticipated changes in aggregate nominal demand was a short-run trade-off to be expected. When anticipations adjust to higher rates of inflation, the initial trade-off is reversed, and the 'natural rate of unemployment' emerges as a long-run magnitude that is determined exclusively be real factors. According to monetarists, and 'expectations adjusted' relation between price level changes and unemployment is represented by a vertical Phillips-curve.

But the monetarist argument does not stop there. The empirical evidence of the coexistence of high inflation and high unemployment has been rationalized by Friedman as ' a transitional problem' from one monetary regime to another, — a 'transition', however, that might last 'for some decades' (Friedman 1977, p. 464f.).

The positively sloped Phillips curve is conjectured to be a phenomenon of a transition of institutional and political arrangements "to a new reality" — and the reality that is suggested is that of some Latin American countries with chronically high inflation rates. I find this rationalization of a positive relation between unemployment and inflation somewhat doubtful for the European case. We should rather pick up Friedman's suggestion, I think, that "such a positive relation may also occur for other reasons".

Structural Disequilibrium

The first oil-price shock of 1973 is mentioned by Friedman as one of the causes that accelerated inflation and — independently of that acceleration — increased unemployment because it directly disrupted productive processes. Now, it is true that this was a particular — or particularly perceived shock, and that it aggravated tremendously a recession already under way in a number of countries. The fundamental modification of "the factors influencing growth and inflation" in the European countries, however, dates pre-1973.

What came to the fore after the decades of post-war reconstruction — but pre-1973 — was, according to the structuralist hypothesis, the coincidence of continuous and deliberately organizeed 'disruptions of productive processes', i.e. structural change, and of increasingly assymmetrical modes of adaptation to changing conditions : A kind of clash between putty requirements and clay responses, if that is the appropriate metaphor in a Dutch context.

In a recent paper, Fitoussi and Georgescu-Roegen (1979) have stressed the continuity of structural change due to technological progress, innovations and re-locations on the supply-side, and to income-related shifts on the demand side. As firms and branches are continuously involved in processes of adaptation to changing conditions, disequilibria and transitions are taken to be the normal state of affairs, and equilibrium is reduced to a conceptual state for the distinction of disequilibrium : "We believe that innovations are the main causes of disequilibrium, whether on the labor market or on other markets". And : "One disequilibrium comes after another so that the long-run equilibrating forces have little chance to come into operation".

Structural change, however, means changing relations between branches and the economy as a whole. The relative shares of branches in total capacity output and/or employment changes. And with structural change in the composition of the labour force the relative share of particular occupational groups may vary as well. If we want to study the effects of these changes on employment and inflation, the meso-economic approach suggests itself. In fact, it becomes imperative. The postulate of a homogeneous macroeconomic state, basic to Keynesian diagnosis and policies, cannot be accepted any longer. In the terminology of Malinvaud, this postulate means in fact that the economy as a whole is considered either a sellers' or a buyers' market. In a situation of deficient effective demand, i.e. excess supplies, it is assumed, strictly speaking, that as soon as one seller is rationed, no buyer is rationed. Obviously, this makes little sense for a real economy. What can, however, be postulated, is this : For any particular commodity market and labour market segment this condition may be assumed to hold, and, moreover, at any one time different markets may show contrary conditions, some being sellers' and other buyers' markets.

Translating these theoretical concepts into empirical ones, we would expect to observe in reality the coexistance in any one empirical ones, we would expect to observe in reality the coexistance in any one cyclical phase of distinct groups of industries characterized by diffferent or even opposed market conditions. Disaggregating the average rate of change of, say, industrial production we would expect to find, next to a group of industries whose rate of change is in fact close to the average, another group of industries whose performance is clearly above, and a third group that is clearly below average. Taking the average as the trend line and considering deviations from trend, we might call these three groups 1. the (relatively) expanding), 2. the average, and 3. the (relatively) declining group. The first and the third group may not be related to sellers' and to buyers' markets respectively.

I have shown elsewhere (Willke 1978) empirically for the case of Germany that what is commonly perceived — and politically treated — as the business cycle in fact consists in a variety of branch cycles. These show a particular pattern of variation relative to the usual macroeconomic indicator which, of course, represents a weighted average of a number of particular movements. The mean rate of change of industrial production or the mean degree of capacity utilization signify close to nothing. For the years 1973 to 1975, I observed a considerable and increasing variance of branches around their respective mean values. In 1974, for instance, when the average

rate of change of industrial production in manufacturing fell
2.1 per cent the various branches ranged between a fall of 1.40
per cent for glass production and an 8 per cent increase for
iron and steel.

Grouping similarly performing branches together into the
before-mentioned three broad categories – (relatively)
expanding, average (stagnating) and (relatively) declining
groups of branches – may provide an idea of the magnitude and
development of the 'structural disequilibrium' within the
cycle.

Cyclical fluctuations and structural change combine to
create a permanent state of partial disequilibria and of
uncertainty. Economic decision units, i.e. firms and
households, have to adapt accordingly. It should be noticed
that even in a strongly depressed period like that of 1974-75,
there is still a considerable group of branches that shows a
positive rate of change of production. Conversely, it should be
expected that even in boom phases, a certain group of branches
will have negative rates of production growth. The dispersion
of branches around the mean varies during the cycle; it is
higher in peak and trough years and lower in between.

What emerges from these facts is that disequilibrium – or
more precisely : partial disequilibria in various branches – is
not a negligeable transitional phenomenon but should be
considered the normal state of affairs. There is a constant
flow of disequilibrating factors : technical change and product
innovation, changing tastes and demand shifts, a changing
international division of labour, political shocks, etc.

It is the differential incidence of novelties and of all
other changes in demand and supply conditions that produces a
certain variance between the developments of different branches
– in other words : structural disequilibrium. This entails
continuous disruptions in established patterns of production
and employment. In principle, of course, we would not need to
worry about the existence and effects of structural
disequilibrium if the adjustments of economic decision units to
imbalances were fast and symmetrical in tight and loose
markets. Unfortunately, however, they are not.

What we observe are asymmetrical modes of adaptation.
Asymmetry is here interpreted as a form of resistance to undo
or dismantle what the agents concerned consider achievements :
a once achieved level of real wages, a certain level of prices,
invested capacity etc. It is the expression of a certain
irreversibility of movements in economic space.

Three types of asymmetries in particular are relevant for
the generation of unemployment and inflation in structural
disequilibrium :

- asymmetry concerning processes of accumulation and decumulation;
- asymmetries concerning upward and downward adjustments of prices (wages) and quantities, and
- asymmetries concerning participation rates of particular labour market groups in expansion and contraction.

The first asymmetry is important when we abandon the Keynesian vantage point of considering only variations in effective demand within the limits of existing and structurally 'right' capacities. As Scitovsky has argued, there are "asymmetrical consequences of going beyond those limits". The third asymmetry is important when fluctuations in business activity and structural change imply regional displacements and re-allocations. Given the limitations of this paper, however, I do not wish to deal with the first two points, but rather to concentrate of the effects of the main asymmetry, namely that of prices (wages) and quantities – which, incidentally, is also relevant for the disequilibrium theories of unemployment, as mentioned earlier.

The predominance of upward price and wage adjustments over quantity adjustments has been rationalized in various ways, e.g. as an effect of production adjustment costs, of labour as a quasi fixed factor, and of uncertainty. Given uncertainty and incomplete information, a firm that is confronted with an unanticipated increase in the demand for its product will not know whether this expansion is special to it, a demand shift towards the products of its branch or pervasive throughout the economy as a result of nominal demand expansion. The firm will also not know whether it is faced with a transient acceleration or a persistent favourable shift in the demand for its product. A rational reaction of the firm under uncertainty will be to first adjust prices upwardly and possibly put in a few extra shifts but defer building up of new capacities and hiring of additional labour –until the increase will have proved to be persistent.

The downward rigidity of prices is largely determined by the downward stickiness of wages which in turn may be attributed to institutional factors, implicit contracts (risk shifting), real wage resistence and other factors. The result of this asymmetry of price-quantity adjustments is the well known kinky supply curve, – where the kink, however, is not a full capacity output but at the point of actual utilization.

We can formalise the adaptation of supply in the commodity market i (ΔS_i) in response to a change in effective demand for commodity i(Δd_i) by the following equation :

(1) $\Delta s_i = \lambda_i \Delta d_i$ where

(2) $\lambda = k_i + h_i \delta_i$ $1 \geqslant h \geqslant k \ o$
        $\delta_i = 0 \ \text{for} \ \Delta d_i \ 0$ $s_i = k_i \Delta d_i$
        $\delta_i = 1 \ \text{for} \ \Delta d_i \ 0$ $s_i = (k_i + h_i) \Delta d_i$

Total supply change, then, is

(3) $\Delta S = \sum\limits_{\substack{i=1 \\ f=1}}^{n} \Delta s_i$

which can be decomposed into two sums, the first one
representing all markets with excess demand, and the second one
representing all markets with deficient demand :

(4) $\Delta S = \sum\limits_{i=1}^{} k_i \Delta d_i - \sum\limits_{j=n-j+1}^{} (k_j + h_j) \Delta d_j$

where d^+ denotes deficient demands.
The right hand side of equation (4) represents aggregate demand
change, and the left hand side is the aggregate supply change.
Let us assume that in any given situation a change in the level
and composition of aggregate effective demand occurs such that
in a number of markets (i = 1 to n-j) we get positive demand
changes, and in the other markets (j = n-j+1 to n) we get
negative demand changes. The supply reaction is mainly
determined by the negative demand changes (Δd_j^+), given that
$h \geqslant k$.

To the extent, therefore, that a variation in aggregate
effective demand — whether endogenous or policy induced —
creates or aggravates structural disequilibrium, and runs into
kinked firm or market supply curves, we would expect a very
feeble reaction of aggregate supply, an increase in
inflationary pressures, and possibly redundancies in markets
that are negatively affected by a demand shift.

Another demonstration of the implications of this
structuralist approach is to start from a general and
structural equilibrium — assuming that such a thing exists in a
state of 'suspended animation'. If we now introduce
'animation', i.e. a change in pattern of aggregate demand that
leaves its level unchanged ($\Sigma \Delta d_i + \Sigma \Delta d_j = 0$) then obviously a
macroeconomic approach would signal no change whereas the
structuralist approach would signal the simultaneous
intensification of both inflation and unemployment. In markets
with negative demand increases (deficient demand : the K-

sector) we would expect redundancies of factors, and in markets with positive demand increases (excess demand : the C-sector) we would expect inflationary pressures.

The conclusion from this reasoning — which could and should, of course, be expanded — is that the occurrence, and any aggravation, of structural disequilibrium causes an increase in both the level of unemployment and of prices. It is further concluded that "at the source of any unemployment, one finds structural change". (Fitoussi, Georgescu-Roegen, p. 11). As structural change is a continuous process, we would expect unemployment to be persistent, — and be accompanied by inflation.

By way of illustration, I could mention the case of Italy where the rate of inflation at present is around 20 per cent, unemployment is still increasing, and aggregate effective demand is expanding moderately. Some branches like tourist services or personal security services are increasing while Fiat has announced, or threatened, to lay off some 28,000 workers because of a declining demand for automobiles.

This leads us more or less directly to the question of the choices for economic policy in a situation of structural disequilibrium.

Policy Conclusions

Economic policy today can start from four more or less generally accepted assumptions :
- The idea of a non-shifting Phillips-curve has to be rejected; the penalty for an increase in effective demand is higher than a once-and-for-all increase in the rate of inflation.
- There is no such thing as a homogeneous macroeconomic state, nor is there anything like a homogeneous macroeconomic policy. Structural change and demand fluctuations have a differential impact on the various branches, and so does any type of demand management.
- Economic policy is no longer — if it ever was — concerned with influencing or controlling economic variables but has to deal with groups who condition economic outcomes : business groups, labour unions, other political bodies, occupational groups, categories of households (and voters). A heavy element of bargaining and persuasion is therefore involved.
- It is true that market failures exist, — but so do policy failures. Generally speaking, economic policy has failed to live up to the high requirements of anti-cyclical demand management as well as selective demand and supply policies.

The first two assumptions imply that the good old days of mono-causal explanations and corresponding policies are gone. The problem at hand is no longer - if it ever was - one of a deficiency or an excess of aggregate demand which should and could be corrected by government's anticyclical demand management. The problem itself is a complex one given the simultaneity of inflation and unemployment, and it is compounded by the fact that what is held to be "global" demand management does in fact have a structurally differentiated impact. The outcome of applying globally intended but in fact structurally effective measures on a homogeneously perceived but in fact structurally differentiated 'conjuncture' can hardly be, to put it mildly, a controlled one.

The logical consequence of the structuralist diagnosis - and it is the consequence which Fitoussi (1978) draws - is to abandon global demand management, and instead resort to selective policies. He proposes active structural policies of 'reconversion' of productive capacities and of the labour force from declining and stagnating branches to expanding branches thereby reducing the asymmetry which is at the core of the economic policy problem. Government should place incentives for the re-allocation of capital, labour and other resources from the K-sector (the Keynesian sector with deficient demand) to the C-sector (the classical sector with deficient supply). This implies a capacity to reflect about the future and analyse economic trends that determine the "winners" of tomorrow.

Presenting Fitoussi's policy conclusions this way will leave little doubt that I tend to take issue with them. I perfectly agree that these are the logical conclusions to be drawn from the analysis but on the grounds of assumptions 3 and 4 I would prefer to substitute political consequences for the logical ones.

I have little confidence in the capacity of the state, i.e. of civil servants, to pick the winners, and to carry out consistent structural policies of the 'conversion' type. In economic affairs, the state has proved to be "all thumbs and no fingers", and if the market process cannot pick the winners, nobody can.

Given that the core of our problem lies in structural disequilibrium and asymmetrical adaptations, what governments can and should do is to provide a medium-term stable framework and to facilitate adaptations of capital and labour to changing conditions - not by erratic selective policies but by measures that fall into the category of "Ordnungspolitik": reductions of government imposed or sanctioned obstacles to dynamic entrepreneurial behaviour and to innovation, competition policy, improvements in the level and flexibility of education,

training and re-training, facilitation of part-time work etc.
I am aware of the fact that this sounds very pro-market or even 'monetaristic'. I do not intend to propose, however, the demolition of rigidities which are the expression of useful safeguards against the risks of market economies. What I do want to emphasize is that a structuralist diagnosis does not necessarily lead to a 'structuralist' policy menu. Unfortunately, policy failures have to be taken as seriously as market failures.

References

R.J. Barro, H.G. Grossman "A General Disequilibrium Model of Income and Employment", American Economic Review, 1971, pp. 821-93.

A. Coddington, "The Theory of Unemployment Reconsidered", Journal of Economic Literature, Sept. 1978.

Commission of the European Communities, The Economic Situation of the Community.

J.P. Fitoussi, "Inflation et Chômage. L'impossible régulation conjoncturelle d'un dés-équilibre structurelle", Cahiers Francais, May-June 1978.

J.P. Fitoussi, N. Georgescu-Roegen, "Structure and Involuntary Unemployment", Bureau d'Economie Théorique et Applique. Université Louis Pasteur, Strasbourg.

M. Friedman, "Inflation and Unemployment", Journal of Political Economy, 1977, pp. 451-472.

T.W. Hutchison, Keynes versus the 'Keynesians', IEA Hobart Paperback No. 11, London.

A. Maddison, "Western Economic Performance in the 1970s: A Perspective and Assessment", Banca Nazionale del Lavoro Quarterly Review, Sept. 1980, pp. 247-289.

A. Malinvaud, The Theory of Unemployment Reconsidered, London 1977.

T. Negishi, Microeconomic Foundations of Keynesian Macroeconomics, Amsterdam, 1979.

T. Scitovsky, "Asymmetries in Economics", Scottish Journal of Political Economy, 1978, pp. 227-237.

G. Willke, Globalsteuerung und gespaltene Konjunktur. Stabilisierungspolitik bei sektoral differenziertem Zyklus, Stuttgart, Klett-Cotta 1978.

COMMENTS ON WILLKE'S PAPER

J.C. Siebrand, Erasmus University, Rotterdam

Professor Willke's presentation of the structuralist view of unemployment adds a new dimension to our discussion. It highlights the theoretical background of the need for disaggregation. The main point of his paper is that aggregation obscures the fundamental adjustment problems of our economies. Disaggregation or not is not merely a matter of detail.

A meso level of aggregation is essential to analyze the causes of the simultaneous existence of unemployment and inflation. The novelty in the structuralist approach is the stress on the defective adjustments in different segments of the product market and the labour market, and the aggregate consequences of asymmetric reactions to excess demand and excess supply. The arguments for this vision are mainly borrowed from modern disequilibrium analysis.

The main arguments are:
a. the existence of uncertainties, combined with external shocks, such as innovation;
b. price inflexibility, especially downwards;
c. quantity constraints, both per market and between markets;
d. asymmetries.

The existence of uncertainties implies that economic agents have to base their decisions on incomplete information. They will have to form expectations, which they can update from period to period. They may have to decide which external changes are temporal and which are structural in this process. Agents will be aware of the fact that present decisions may constitute constraints on their future activities, also if these decisions are based on wrong anticipations. These considerations imply that agents will as a rule adjust only gradually to external changes. Many of their responses will be lagged. Another factor Willke might have mentioned in this respect are adjustment costs.

If this picture of economic life is realistic the model of perfect competition is less adequate for empirical analysis of price and quantity adjustment. Kuipers reminded us correctly of Arrow's argument that it is not at all clear who changes prices under perfect competition.

Let us consider the case of <u>ex ante</u> excess supply.

Willke hardly needs new arguments for downward inflexibility or prices. The general point seems to be that you know what you lose, but you do not know what you gain by lowering prices. The discussion about depreciation of the guilder in this conference may act as an example of reluctance with respect to downward price adjustment.

Willke uses Scitovsky's kinked supply-curve analysis to study price reactions to demand changes, but I do not find this analysis very illuminating, as it lacks a dynamic setting.

I also have my doubts about Willke's suggestion that upward price flexibility is probable in case of ex ante excess demand. If, in the short run, imperfect rather than perfect competition is the rule, the short term price elasticity of demand may be rather low. Full adjustment of prices may then call for large price fluctuations. This may be damaging for future sales if competitors do not act similarly. Their possible behaviour may determine the amount of upward price adjustment. Potential foreign competition seems very relevant for Dutch suppliers. Sectors in which no such danger exists do not seem to fear upward price adjustment to cost increases, as their domestic competitors can be trusted to be in the same position. The profit squeeze in other Dutch sectors can for a substantial part be explained by the rapid increase of domestic costs relative to foreign prices. In spite of the reluctance of some sectors to upward price adjustment, it seems fair to conclude that, given the more general downward rigidity of prices, that aggregate prices will tend to be biased upwards, compared to the level they would have, if full adjustment in all markets were possible.

Price inflexibility has direct consequences for quantity adjustment. Standard disequilibrium theory states that transactions tend to the minimum of demand and supply if prices are rigid. Hansen has sketched, and Muellbauer has formalized the aggregate situation if excess demand exists in some submarkets, and excess supply in others. Aggregate transactions can then be proven to lie below the minimum of aggregate demand and aggregate supply, and the more so if excess demand and excess supply are more equally distributed over submarkets.

The obvious result is a downward bias in aggregate quantities, which bias is reinforced if interactions between markets are taken into account. If these deviations from standard equilibrium analysis are realistic, the question arises how we should adjust our analytical framework for economic policy. The proportions of the ideal model are not difficult to outline. It would describe the dynamic adjustment behaviour of different sectors of the economy at a low level of aggregation. It would generate both the expectations and the decisions of relevant agents in several submarkets, together with the confrontation of these plans in those markets. Such confrontations might lead to rationing if price adjustment to initial inconsistency in plans of different agents would be insufficient. Spill-overs between markets could also occur.

I believe that for the near future the construction of such models is hardly feasible, because of the theoretical and practical difficulties involved. To what extent can we make do with existing systems for the time being?

The prospects for explicit disequilibrium analysis may be better at the macro level. Models that really describe dynamic adjustment behaviour are far from easy to implement, but not necessarily completely out of the question. Simpler systems based on the neo-classical modelling of notional demand and supply, explicit disequilibrium interactions between markets, and mixed aggregate regimes (compromising between demand and supply) can be operational according to my partial experience in this area. It should not be forgotten, of course, that many empirical macro models do contain a number of disequilibrium elements on an ad hoc base.

The existing sectoral models are perhaps also less inadequate than one would think. Many differential developments of sectors may just follow from different income and price elasticities, given smoothly changing technological structures. Structural change is for a large part endogeneous if this is true. This may even hold for a part of the innovations. Therefore I believe that Willke overstates the external character of structural "shocks". In reality the bulk of the uncertainty may lie in foreign supply. Structural changes in this supply may to a considerable extent be explained in a larger "equilibrium" setting.

Summarizing, I agree in principle with the views presented by Willke, but perhaps the issues are somewhat less dramatic than presented.

His policy propositions are rather poor in my view. I fully agree that government planning is hardly a solution because government lacks both foresight and insight. But reliance on "Ordnungspolitik" such as stimulation of competition and re-education does not seem very promising. I would have expected suggestions like helping quantities to adjust upwards, such as subsidizing growth as Baumol proposed in the sixties, or stimulating prices to adjust downwards. Wage- and price-policies might be helpful in this respect. Another type of measure might be subsidies or taxes to correct inadequate prices.

Finally, I would like to stress a point that seems rather important to me. If some sectors have to adjust upwards and others downwards the process of adjustment is very difficult in a situation of stagnation or contraction, because of quite a number of downward rigidities. Reshuffling is far easier in a situation of expansion. National authorities in almost all industrial countries seem to hope that they can increase their international market share by deflationary policies. Their combined action frustrates the prospects for an overall increase in world demand which would be really helpful, as it would create the circumstances for adjustment in expansion. If we put this situation in the wider perspective of the non-spent oil dollars and the growing problems for developing countries I think proposals like those of the Brandt commission deserve serious study.

Knoester and Van Sinderen demonstrated the prohibitive effects of additional spending on a national scale. A part of these problems might be avoided by a simultaneous move of the OECD countries. If this is true, a combined effort to boost world trade might contribute substantially to the solution of the present unemployment problems.

COMMENTS ON WILLKE'S PAPER

Reinold H. van Til, Ministry of Social Affairs, The Hague.

Let me first say that in many respects I can agree with Willke's analysis and policy conclusions, not so much because the structuralist diagnosis reveals surprising truths but more because the structuralist propositions seem so plain and evident. Denying them seems hardly possible. That everything is in motion, in a state of flux, that a state of equilibrium is never attained (at least not visible) is a very old truth, which if I am not mistaken goes back to a very old Greek philosopher.

At the same time I must confess that the structuralist diagnosis of the unemployment situation does not bring me much further. In fact the paper does not deal with the unemployment problem, but with the trade-off between unemployment and inflation. I think we must separate the problem of unemployment and of inflation. Of course unemployment is a structural problem in the sense Willke uses that term. It may be sensible to have a more disaggregated analysis of macroeconomic phenomena, at least if we believe that we cannot grasp the problem at a higher level of aggregation. In this regard I have several questions and remarks. First of all I would like to hear what are the conclusions of a disaggregated analysis of the employment problem that contradict conclusions reached by an analysis at the macroeconomic level. Secondly, why do structuralists not go further than the meso level. Why not analyse the behaviour of individual agents. Of course we will quickly reach the point of not seeing the wood for the trees. Thirdly, leaving aside the importance of a disaggregated analysis for theoretical reasons, I have serious doubts about the relevancy of the structuralist analysis for economic policy. For instance, has the vintage approach of investment guided us to different policy conclusions than those of a conjunctural structural model based on a homogeneous conception of capital. Fourthly, I cannot discover what is new in the structuralist paradigm as presented by Willke.

Honestly said I thought that the structuralist analysis as an alternative to Keynesian and classical thinking pretends more than just giving an analysis at a more disaggregated level. I recall the structuralist monetarist controversy about inflation in Latin America. The structuralist criticism against current economic thinking has been that it did not offer a real remedy for the problem of inflation. Monetarists and Keynesians alike attack symptoms and do not cure the disease. What is at stake according to the structuralists is more fundamental. It has to do with our economic system. Transforming that interpretation to the employment problem and the discussions here one may wonder why there are so many self imposed contraints of a political, economic and institutional character. The question why we are not able to solve the unemployment problem because of these constraints seems at least as interesting as the unemployment problem itself. What we have heard these days implies scepticism about the importance of several instruments of economic policy. Kessler calls monetary policy merely conditional. I think that is a tricky word. De Galan does not expect much substantive effect from labour market policies, because of important institutional and social constraints. From expansionary policies through the government budget nothing is expected because of the working of negative multipliers. At the same time the outcome of budget negotiations seems necessarily to imply an upward trend in taxes and expenditures. Taking everything together there is a strong tendency to minimize the possible contribution of various instruments of economic policy and to isolate the employment problem to - one can choose - the level of real wages, the profit squeeze, the malfunctioning of the labour market, the oil crisis etc. One may worry about the fact that the economic profession has not given a clearcut answer about what should be done. While the discussions go on one hopes that the unemployment problem is solved by a bio external shock.

THE PROFITS SQUEEZE, UNEMPLOYMENT AND POLICY : A MARXIST APPROACH

John Harrison, Thames Polytechnic

THE PROFITS SQUEEZE
Facts

It is now generally acknowledged that profit rates in all major advanced-capitalist countries have declined considerably from the levels of the mid sixties. All serious studies of this phenomenon also show two other features which are perhaps less well recognised. One is that, with the apparent exception of France, this decline pre-dates the oil crisis and the crash of 1974. The other is that the fall in the profit rate prior to 1974 is to be explained, in a statistical sense, primarily by a fall in the share of profits in value added, rather than by a rise in the capital/output ratio. There is some variation between countries here, but a world series - constructed as a weighted average of the leading capitalist powers - would undoubtedly show that the change in the profit share dominated that in the rate (See e.g. Clark and Williams, Feldstein and Summers, Delestre and Mairesse, National Income statistics of Japan, Hill).

To put this in marxist terminology, the evidence shows overwhelmingly that profits fell prior to the mid-seventies because of a fall in the rate of exploitation, rather than a rise in the organic composition of capital.

Significance of the Squeeze

There is less agreement as to the significance of the profits squeeze. Some commentators accord it little importance (eg. OECD, 1977), others - notably capitalist organizations (eg. the British CBI) and Marxists (eg. Mandel, Glyn and Harrison) - regard it as central to recent economic difficulties. It is perhaps not surprising that there should be fundamental disagreements here - it is not an issue which can be settled by any 'simple' appeal to evidence; rather it depends on one's underlying view as to the nature and dynamics of capitalism.

Here I will simply state my view, which is that, whilst small variations in a reasonably 'adequate' rate of return are not necessarily of much import, a substantial decline to a level which capital finds unacceptably low has serious implications for the reproduction of the system. It discourages accumulation - which is the basic motor of capitalism - and makes the system far more vulnerable to the kinds of shocks and dislocations which inevitably occur from time to time.

I would thus argue that the decline in profits is the fundamental cause of the emergence in the seventies of high levels of inflation followed by mass unemployment (and their subsequent stubborn persistence). This does not imply that so-called 'random shocks' (eg. the oil crises), 'policy errors' (eg. 'excessive' reflation in the early seventies) and other long-term 'structural' developments (e.g. decline of the U.S. and hence the dollar) were not important in the timing, form and severity of the present crisis. But I would argue that these other factors were ultimately secondary, in that a more healthy capitalism could probably have adjusted to them without too much disruption; and that the inherently unhealthy state of advanced capitalism by the early seventies meant that it was heading for trouble regardless of OPEC etc.

Causes of the Squeeze

Since this conference is centered around the appropriateness of the 'Vintaf' model, it seems appropriate to express my basic argument in terms of a simple clay/clay vintage model. (This is done intuitively rather than formally).

In such model, a given rate and form of accumulation will, in a situation of full employment, entail and generate a certain rate of growth of real wages, determined by the rate of technical progress and the rate of growth of the labour force. The rate and form of accumulation determines the demand for 'additional' labour provided 'exogenously'. The rest can be provided only by the scrapping of older vintages and the consequent release of workers. The rate of technical progress (at the time of the installation of the oldest vintages in operation) determines the growth in real wages required to render sufficient old machines unprofitable to release enough workers to operate all new ones.

It is obviously possible to envisage an equilibrium situation in which the rate of accumulation, rate of growth of the labour force and rate of technical progress are such as to maintain a constant profit share and full employment. This can be regarded as a highly stylised description of Western Europe and Japan in the early sixties.

Now suppose a reduction in the rate of growth of the labour force occurs. If the old pattern of accumulation continues (and technical progress does not accelerate) then scrapping must accelerate and the share of profits decline. Further, unless workers savings rise more than proportionately to incomes, the higher ratio of accumulation to profits implies an increase in overall demand which, in a situation of full employment, will tend to generate inflation.

This can be regarded as a highly stylised description of Western Europe and Japan in the late sixties and early seventies. (The reduction in the rate of growth of the labour force resulting primarily from the rundown of unemployment in peasant agriculture and the tightening of immigration controls).

Whilst I obviously cannot 'prove' in any simple sense that this is what took place, I would argue that it is the most plausible account of underlying mechanisms consistent with the factors. How else can the generalised fall in the profit share (faster growth of real wages than of productivity) and acceleration of prices to be explained? Plausible ad hoc explanations can be constructed for particular countries, but they fail to account for the generalized nature of the phenomenon. Increased trade union militancy – which is sometimes offered as a general explantion – is unsatisfactory on two counts : it 'hangs in the air' in that, in the absence of underlying labour shortage, it is hard to see why it should be a generalized development across countries; and, in the absence of other factors, can only explain an acceleration of money wages, not of real wages.

Neo-classical Marxism?

In his closing remarks at the Conference, Angus Maddison described my approach – semi – seriously, I think – as 'neo-classical Marxism'. There is obviously some justification for the label, but it may be worth saying briefly why I think that in two important respects it is marxist and non neo-classical.

(1)   It is very classically marxist in seeing crisis resulting falling profits, which in turn result from over-accumulation i.e. a rate of accumulation (pushed on capitalists by competition) which is in excess of that which the system can sustain. It differs from more traditional marxist accounts only in seeing the mechanism as overaccumulation in relation to the labour supply, and hence a bidding down of the profit share, rather than a rise in the organic composition, and hence a reduction in the profit rate, with a constant or rising profit share.

(2)   It is anti- neo-classical in implicitly assuming non-smooth adjustment. (At the very least no self-respecting neo-classical would be seen dead with a clay/clay vintage model).

POLICY IMPLICATIONS

Most discussions about policy, including those at this conference concern options available to the state which do not step beyond (at least most of) the existing structural parameters of capitalism. They are about how to create an economic environment in which capital will once more find it worthwhile to accumulate at a pace which generates full employment and permits steady rises in living standards. I shall refer to this issue as 'policies for capital'.

There are also discussions within the labour movement which begin from workers' immediate interests (employment, living standards etc.) and seek policies to protect these interests which may involve altering some of the structural parameters of the system. I shall refer to these options as 'policies for labour'.

Policies for Capital

With profits hit before the onset of recession, and markets weak since the 1974 crash, the restoration of adequate conditions for sustained accumulation requires an improvement in both the conditions for producing surplus value (roughly, full employment profit ability) and those for realizing it (roughly, effective demand). The fundamental problem for the authorities is that policies which work to improve one of these conditions simultaneously work to worsen the other. Reflation, for example, improves realisation conditions but, by reducing unemployment and strenghthening the working class, makes it harder to achieve an improvement in production conditions.

The 'crisis of Keynesianism' is fundamentally a result of the inadequacy of simply stimulating realization conditions when production conditions are also poor. Reflation leads primarily to speculation and price acceleration rather than to enhanced accumulation The mini-boom of 1972-73 is a good example. The main Keynesian 'solution' to production conditions in current vogue – incomes policy – is increasingly correctly seen as politically unworkable given the present balance of class forces (see e.g. OECD 1977). Hence the rise of monetarism.

Monetarism focuses almost exclusively on the conditions for producing surplus value. As a practical policy, shorn of its ideological floss, it is in essence simply deflation. The idea is to create a slump and thereby weed out low efficiency producers, galvanise management and, most importantly, break the organised working class so as to raise the rate of exploitation. Since there are the functions seen by marxism as being performed by classic, 'unengineered' slumps, monetarism can polemically be described as right wing marxism.

If monetarism could succeed in weakening the working class enough to permit a subsequent expansion, with the entailed reduction in unemployment, whilst maintaining an adequate rate of exploitation (and reasonable price stability) then it could in principle lay the basis for a new boom. Whether it can do so in practice depends eventually on political factors : pressure from capital (which is hit by the slump in the short run) and, more importantly, from the labour movement.

Policies for Labour

The dominant alternative to the above policies within the labour movement is that associated with the left-wing of social democracy and certain 'EuroCommunist' parties. Its' essentials are reflation together with various forms of 'supply side intervention' to promote modernization and investment to ensure employment and growth. The measures advocated range from 'soft' (eg. investment grants and other carrots) to 'hard' (compulsory planning agreements, directives to invest and other sticks).

Recent experience has, I think, shown that use of 'soft' measures does not achieve much in the present economic climate. The 'hardest' measures could in principle work (this is obviously a tautology in the case of directives) but would involve depriving capital of the right to make major decisions over economic activity (investment, employment, location etc.). My view is that capital would not accept this process of de facto euthanasia voluntarily, and would fight back by every means possible (as in Chile). It would have a good many powerful weapons at its disposal so long as it retained de facto control over the means of production. The most effective way to minimise this resistance would be sharp expropriation, backed up by the widest possible mass mobilization. I believe that the winning of support for such a programme offers the only real way forward for workers' parties.

REFERENCES

T.A. Clark and N.P. Williams, 'Measures of Real Profitability', Bank of England Quarterly Bulletin, London, December, 1978.

Confederation of British Industry, The Road to Recovery, London, 1976.

H. Delestre and H. Mairesse, La Rentabilité des Societé Privées en France 1956-75, INSEE, Paris, 1977.

A. Glyn and J. Harrison, The British Economic Disaster, London, 1980.

T.P. Hill, Profits and Rates of Return, OECD, Paris 1979.

E. Mandel, Late Capitalism, London, 1975.

National Income Accounts of Japan, various issues, Tokyo and London.

Organization for Economic Co-operation and Development, Towards Full Employment and Price Stability, Paris, 1977.

For Product Safety Concerns and Information please contact our EU
representative GPSR@taylorandfrancis.com Taylor & Francis Verlag GmbH,
Kaufingerstraße 24, 80331 München, Germany

Printed and bound by CPI Group (UK) Ltd, Croydon, CR0 4YY
08/05/2025
01864441-0003